Sweet Friendship

RACHEL RAE ANDERSON

KW
KingdomWinds
PUBLISHING

Copyright © 2023 by Rachel Anderson

All rights reserved. No part of this publication may be reproduced, distributed, or transmitted in any form or by any means, including photocopying, recording, or other electronic or mechanical methods, without the prior written permission of the publisher, except in the case of brief quotations embodied in critical reviews and certain other noncommercial uses permitted by copyright law. For permission requests, write to the publisher at **publishing@kingdomwinds.com**.

Unless otherwise indicated, all Scripture references are taken from the Holy Bible, New International Version®, NIV® Copyright © 1973, 1978, 1984, 2011 by Biblica, Inc.® Used by permission. All rights reserved worldwide.

First Edition, 2023
ISBN 10:978-1-64590-041-2
Published by Kingdom Winds Publishing.
www.kingdomwinds.com
publishing@kingdomwinds.com
Printed in the United States of America.

Table of Contents

Introduction — 4

Week 1: Friending — 5
- Week 1, Day One — 6
- Week 1, Day Two — 9
- Week 1, Day Three — 12
- Week 1, Day Four — 15
- Week 1, Day Five — 18

Week 2: Sacrificial Love — 22
- Week 2, Day One — 23
- Week 2, Day Two — 26
- Week 2, Day Three — 29
- Week 2, Day Four — 32
- Week 2, Day Five — 35

Week 3: Loyally Committed — 38
- Week 3, Day One — 39
- Week 3, Day Two — 43
- Week 3, Day Three — 47
- Week 3, Day Four — 51
- Week 3, Day Five — 56

Week 4: Friendship Pillars — 60
- Week 4, Day One — 61
- Week 4, Day Two — 67
- Week 4, Day Three — 72
- Week 4, Day Four — 77
- Week 4, Day Five — 81

Week 5: Wisdom Unlocked — 86
- Week 5, Day One — 87
- Week 5, Day Two — 89
- Week 5, Day Three — 91
- Week 5, Day Four — 93

Conclusion — 95

Sweet Friendship Cupcakes — 96

Friendship.

That word likely elicits a range of emotions for you. The longing for amazing friends. The heartache of past friendships ending harshly. The soul-longing for people that get you and want to do life with you. The hope for people to come into your life, making it more joyful and fun.

We all long for friendship, and we assume that all other women have it. And while many women experience the sweetness of friendship, there are just as many who are lonely in a crowd of women, desperate for people to laugh with. I've been in both spaces mentioned, blessed with beautiful friendship and longing for people to live life with. There is no perfect friendship. But there is a sweetness to two imperfect people choosing to walk life arm in arm. It's a gift to treasure. But this gift doesn't just happen; it requires vulnerability and intentionality. The risk is great, but the reward is greater. Let's dig into the Scriptures and see just what the Bible shows us about friendship. There is no greater guidebook for life and no greater source of wisdom.

Rae

FRIENDING

I am looking forward to diving deep into friendships, relationships, and all that God will teach us in this study. This week we are going to focus on the state of friendships in our lives: evaluating where we are, where we are going, and our hopes for what is to come. Investing in this week's questions and really evaluating where we are right now will set us up for amazing things in the weeks to come. This week let's meditate on Proverbs 27:9.

VERSE

"Just as lotions and fragrance give sensual delight, a sweet friendship refreshes the soul." Proverbs 27:9, MSG

CHALLENGE

This week I challenge you to think about a friendship in which you would like to continue investing. It could be a relationship that is still new or one that you have been investing in for quite some time. We will spend the week praying for this friend. Praying for her dreams, health, family, faith walk, and anything in her life where she needs God to move in mighty ways. This week, we are going to love a friend through prayer. If you don't have a friend to pray for, spend the week praying for God to open your eyes to the women around you and to provide wisdom as you proceed. There are likely people in your circle; it's a matter of His providing direction on who and what's next.

Week 1
Day One

Learn

"Just as lotions and fragrance give sensual delight, a sweet friendship refreshes the soul." Proverbs 27:9, MSG

Challenge

This week, I challenge you to think about a friendship in which you would like to continue investing. It could be a relationship that is still new or one that you have been investing in for quite some time. We will spend the week praying for this friend. Praying for her dreams, health, family, faith walk, and anything in her life where she needs God to move in mighty ways. This week, we are going to love a friend through prayer. If you don't have a friend to pray for, spend the week praying for God to open your eyes to the women around you and to provide wisdom as you proceed. There are likely people in your circle; it's a matter of His providing direction on who and what's next.

Before we do a deep dive into all the Bible has to share with us, let's first assess our current state of things. Think about friendships in your life, past and present. For some of us, friendships have been sweet and wonderful, but for others, they have left us injured and on guard. Let's take some time to look at friendship in our lives.

> › Do you have, or have you had, a friendship that was good?
> › Are you still friends?
> › Is it still good?

› What about this friendship that made you qualify it as good?

Now we are going to process friendships that turned sour. This one may hurt a little, and I'm sorry we are going here, but so much can be learned from past experiences. Bear with me as we process this for a short time.

› Do you have, or have you had, a friendship that turned sour?
› Are you still friends?
› Is it still sour, or did things change?
› What qualities made that friendship not good?
› Is there anything you could have done differently?

Take a moment and pray for this friend, regardless of the relationship status today. This person once mattered to you, and prayer is such a powerful act of love. Lift her to your Heavenly Father and give any of that mess to Him. We will inevitably carry the hurts of past friendships with us, but we can pursue healing through communion with God.

Pray and process the above. The longing in our hearts for relationship is rooted in our longing for Christ. As we embark on this journey, we need to lean into the only One who can satisfy. Prayer and Truth are key in the weeks to come.

What are your hopes and desires for friendship right now?

Maybe it's the longing for a sweet friend, or maybe it's a desire to strengthen current friendships that don't have that depth yet. Whatever it is, take time to note that and then pray intentionally about it. Our God wants us to take our longings to Him in prayer, so let's invite Him in.

> *"...but in everything, through prayer and petition **with thanksgiving**, present your requests to God." Philippians 4:6, **CSB**.*

God loves community among believers; He wants to help you find people to do life with. We see Jesus model community as He ministered with the disciples. Biblical friendship isn't just something we long for; it's something Christ desires for us as well.

> *"As iron sharpens iron, so one person sharpens another." Proverbs 27:17, **NASB***

READ > ANALYZE > APPLY

Read Ecclesiastes 4:1–12.

> When reading this passage, what stands out to you as it pertains to community and friendship?

> Are you focusing your time and investment on oppressive, envious, and meaningless pursuits?

> If so, where and how? What could you be focusing on instead?

> What do you think a "cord of three strands" friendship looks like? Write down the benefits mentioned in this passage.

> Do you have friendships where inviting God in would make the relationship stronger? In what practical ways could you invite God into that relationship?

Week 1
Day Two

Learn

> *"Just as lotions and fragrance give sensual delight, a sweet friendship refreshes the soul."* Proverbs 27:9, MSG

Challenge

This week we are praying for a friend. Praying for her dreams, health, family, faith walk, and anything in her life where she needs God to move in mighty ways. We are going to spend the week loving a friend through prayer.

Friendship can be such a wonderful blessing. It offers us support and connection and such a sweet way of doing life, but it can also be the source of heartache and pain. For some of us, the word friendship is more synonymous with disappointment and pain than connection and sweetness. As we pursue relationship and friendship, vulnerability is required, and ultimately it is a risky endeavor, one that has the potential to pay off greatly but also the opportunity for heartache and disappointment.

Over the next few days, we are going to take a look at the pain unhealthy friendships can bring. We discuss the yucky stuff, not because we want to dwell on what can go wrong, but because it offers insight and wisdom. If we desire to pursue Godly friendship, we need an understanding of relationships that are out of that alignment. This offers us the freedom to pursue friendship that will build us up and point us to Christ.

As we dive in, we will be discussing Christian friends. Some of this will apply to all friendships, but in this particular study, we are seeking to solidify godly friendships, ones that challenge us to be more like Christ. There will be non-believing friends in our lives, and realistically those relationships will be off-balance. They have to be because the driving force of a Christian life is the pursuit of a life that models Christ, but that same motivation doesn't exist in secular friendships. Please don't misread this as my stating that those friendships can't be sweet or amazing; they absolutely can be beautiful, and I have amazing friendships with non-believing friends. But the purpose and security of those relationships is different than that of my Christ-believing friendships.

Years ago, life had me in a season of desiring friendships and relationships outside of my usual circle. I was in a place where much of life was new and different, and seeking out relationships in the new was important. A woman seemed to be in all the same places as me, we had similar weekly schedules, and life had us in proximity to one another quite regularly. We started interacting during this season and became friends. It became apparent after some time together that I left our interactions completely drained. One day it all clicked, and I realized she was a friend that required too much of me, taking but not giving back. While I still love her dearly, it was obvious that no matter how much I cared for her, I needed to take a step back from that relationship.

Ultimately, friendship shouldn't be so ill-balanced on the regular. Seasons will come where a friend's life will be experiencing struggles, and they most definitely will take more during that season. This offers us the opportunity to speak into her heart, encourage her, walk through hard things with her, and be a support. But this shouldn't be the entire framework of a friendship. There should be a balance of sorts, a natural rhythm that allows for give and take.

If you love a person dearly and pursue friendship, but it's a relationship that leaves you drained, then it may be time to pray and evaluate that person's space in your life. All people matter to Christ. They have value and deserve to be treated as such, but sometimes that person needs to not operate in our primary circle.

Read > Analyze > Apply

Read and meditate on Philippians 4:4–9.

> › What is the heart posture in this passage? How are we to pursue God? How do you think the peace of God helps guard our hearts and minds?

> › What does Paul urge us to think about? How might we put this into practice? How could we apply this to relationships?

> › How could the heart's posture and admonition of these verses positively, or negatively, impact your friendships? How can you apply this to the friendship and friend you are praying for?

Week 1
Day Three

Learn

> *"Just as lotions and fragrance give sensual delight, a sweet friendship refreshes the soul."* Proverbs 27:9, MSG

Challenge

This week we are praying for a friend's dreams, health, family, faith walk, and anything in her life where she needs God to move in mighty ways. We are going to spend the week loving a friend through prayer.

I still remember it like it was yesterday. She was that friend that seemed to be everything in one. We laughed and had fun, we shopped together, we did our nails and toes together, we married at about the same time, and we had kids about the same time. Our husbands were friends, and it seemed like the perfect friendship match. But sometimes, what seems perfect isn't.

One day out of nowhere, she disappeared for many months. Phone calls and texts weren't returned, and just like that, it all changed. I found it odd and couldn't quite wrap my head around the change. But at the same time, I knew she was struggling with some things, and I figured this was how she needed to cope. Then, after many months of zero contact, one day she called and waltzed back into my life as if nothing happened. She spoke of things I didn't know about and of a life lived with other friends, acting as if I had never been cut out for those months. It stung, but I rolled with it, and things seemed to balance out. We were back to life as friends, with all the good I thought that brought.

The friendship worked for quite some time...then one day, she froze me out again. This time, it was for good. She never called back. She never told me why. She just left. I still don't know why. A whisper of something made it back to me, and if that's why, it was a lie and untrue. A true friend has the courage to ask and dialogue about misunderstandings; they don't just walk away when adversity hits.

The recovery from this heartache took years. As I look back now, I see the cracks in what seemed like an awesome friendship. I see the lack of depth; I see the brokenness in her and the brokenness in me through that relationship. I loved the idea of that friendship. I loved what it could have been, but what it was? That wasn't something to love. When we are in the thick of things, it's easy to miss what's right in front of us. I overlooked the shallow and selfish nature of our interactions. I overlooked the unhealthy patterns, and I overlooked the reality that despite being Christians, there was no Christ in our friendship.

Years later, I can look at the trajectory of our lives today, where life took her and where life took me, and honestly, I'm grateful that God saved me from a friendship that wasn't Christ-centered. Businessman and motivational speaker Jim Rohn once said that "You are the average of the five people you spend the most time with."[1] Had this friend of mine continued to be one of those five people, I might not be exactly where God has me today.

The pain of that wound has healed, and I'm beyond grateful for what God taught me through that experience. God has spent the years since refining me in the most gut-wrenching ways possible, but the people by my side all those years were holding me up and pointing my eyes heavenward. That is the true sign of amazing friends, and such relationships should be the longing cry of our hearts. God-honoring friendships will walk the impossible with you. They will have the hard conversations and point you to Truth, and they will complement all God is trying to do with your life.

---

1 **Rohn, Jim. The Art of Exceptional Living: Your Guide to Gaining Wealth, Enjoying Happiness, and Achieving Unstoppable Daily Progress. Sound Wisdom, 2022.**

READ > ANALYZE > APPLY

Read Colossians 3:12–17.

> What are we instructed to clothe ourselves with?

> What is foundational to all of these virtues?

> What should be the posture of our hearts? Who are we reminded to live for in word and deed?

> How do these verses challenge you in the current state of your friendships? What is one action and/or prayer you can add to live this out?

Week 1
Day Four

Learn

"Just as lotions and fragrance give sensual delight, a sweet friendship refreshes the soul." Proverbs 27:9, MSG

Challenge

This week we are praying for a friend's dreams, health, family, faith walk, and anything in her life where she needs God to move in mighty ways. We are going to spend the week loving a friend through prayer.

Let's take a trip down memory lane...back to high school and then even further back to middle school. What do you remember about those years? For me, it's hands down the tumult of relationships in those years. Middle school particularly was all sorts of rough. I remember my 13th birthday. My parents planned a surprise party for me at a local hotel. My friends and I swam and laughed and then went back to the room for typical middle schoolgirl sleepover chats. Somewhere in the girl talk, things got heated. I spent many a day after that party with no friends to sit with at lunch and no gaggle of girls to call friends. My heart still feels the sting of that rejection. Middle school girls can be savage.

Fast forward many years. I was loving the new group of girlfriends in my life. They were fun and kind — no mean girls here, and things seemed good. It can be so awesome to belong to a diverse and amazing group of friends.. But then one day, pictures started appearing on social media, pictures filled with laughs and fun. They were on a girls' trip, and I wasn't invited. They didn't think of me. With each picture, I felt the sting of not being included.

We have all at one time or another been the one left out, the one rejected, and the one not invited. It's a painful place to be. A place filled with shame and feelings of not being good enough. Convinced that if I were better — funnier, prettier, or more memorable — they would have included me. We can succumb to the lies, the dark thoughts that, if given space, will destroy us. Or we can feel the sting, feel that pain, and then take it to the feet of our Heavenly Father. Easier said than done, but it's the only true salve for a wounded heart.

Christ experienced the ultimate rejection when He was denied, publicly shamed, and then crucified. He experienced all of that as a perfect human being with no wrongdoing or sin to His name. I think at times it can be easy to overlook the enormity of what He endured, the absolute heartache and rejection and shame it brought Him. Yet, for us, He did it all. He forgave Judas who rejected Him; He prayed for and encouraged the disciples in the middle of it all, and He prayed forgiveness for those that know not what they do (Luke 23:34). He suffered with abundant grace. If He could endure all of that, surely He can understand our pain of rejection. He gets it. He endured so much yuck for you because YOU matter to Him. Like big time matter to Him. No amount of rejection or being overlooked can undo that.

When we feel the sting, we need to run to the one who loves us unconditionally. We need to pour over His Truth, what He says about us and who we are. And more importantly, we need to dwell on the Truth of Whose we are. The sting loses its burn when we realize Christ accepts us for who we are as we are. He chose me and you when we were at our absolute worst: dirty, sin-filled people. And He wants to spend time with us, wants us to come to Him in prayer, and wants us to spend our days in communion with Him. He WANTS US. So, we lean in to the One who paid it all.

READ > ANALYZE > APPLY

Read 1 Peter 4:1–11.

> We are urged to live with the same attitude as Jesus. According to this passage, what does that look like?

> How do you think suffering like Christ challenges us to love each other deeply? Pray on how you can love like Christ.

> What are your God-given giftings? Are you using them for His glory?

> What is a practical way that you can apply "living for the will of God" to your friendships?

Week 1
Day Five

Learn

"Just as lotions and fragrance give sensual delight, a sweet friendship refreshes the soul." Proverbs 27:9, MSG

Challenge

This week we are praying for a friend's dreams, health, family, faith walk, and anything in her life where she needs God to move in mighty ways. We are going to spend the week loving a friend through prayer.

Friends, thank you for sticking with me as we dove into the heartache relationship can bring. We know that God has the best hopes for our relationships, and today we are going to look at the sweetness of good friendship. When we invite God into the center of our friendships, the impact on our lives, the lives of our friends, and those we encounter can be monumental. The crux of this, though, is finding people that we can walk with arm in arm as we do life. Earlier this week, we were reminded that friendship can be harsh and harmful, leaving us with the knowledge to wisely pursue relationship.

This is not a pursuit for the faint of heart. As we pursue relationship and friendship, vulnerability is required, and ultimately it is a risky endeavor. It's a risk that has the potential to pay off greatly, but it also creates the opportunity for heartache and disappointment. Much of our Christian life is intended to be lived boldly, so let's pursue friendships with the boldness of Christ but not in a way that leaves us foolishly exposed. Let's be wise as we pursue a godly community of women, changing the world through their love and commitment to one another.

A cord of three strands cannot be broken (Ecclesiastes 4:12). We often hear this verse referred to in the context of marriage, but it applies to friendship as well. If we have God as the foundation, we are already that much stronger in our friendship. Jordan Lee Dooley says it well in a 2017 blog post: "Friending is like loving, rarely easy but always worth it, because it requires much but also returns much."[2] As we embark on this journey towards Godly friendship, we will need to be intentional as we pray, pursue, and invest in relationship.

Read Psalm 133 with me.

> *"How delightfully good when brothers live together in harmony!*
> *It is like fine oil on the head, running down on the beard,*
> *running down Aaron's beard onto his robes. It is like the dew of*
> *Hermon falling on the mountains of Zion. For there the Lord has*
> *appointed the blessing— life forevermore."* **Psalm 133, CSB**

As we read this passage, it paints a picture that's a little hard to understand in today's reality. Not to mention, maybe even unpleasant. Oil running down onto a beard and then clothes? Well, that feels cringe-worthy to me. Oil is greasy and hard to clean off of hair and skin; to clean it off clothes is difficult and usually involves stains. But in this passage, it appears to be a good thing. Let's unpack this a bit.

The oil that I just described so lovingly is in reference to anointing oil. Anointing oil is a holy thing; it was precious and used to anoint the First High Priest. It was used only for those serving the Lord. This holy oil, used only for the most devoted servants of Christ, is being described here in relation to whole living. When we live in precious unity with our brothers and sisters in Christ, it is a uniquely special thing, so special that it's as if the most sacred oil, reserved only for the Lord's anointing, is being poured out onto our relationship. It's a holy and precious thing to be appreciated for the specialness it brings.

Even better, this precious oil, when poured out onto our relationship, then flows down. It flows down to the relationships, people, and others in proximity to this uniquely special and unified whole. Similar to the sticky, greasy oil that I lamented trying to clean off clothes, hair, and skin, this will stick to all it flows onto. The impact of God's people living in unity is exponential. This is how the world will see that a life lived wholly devoted to Christ is uniquely special.

As we dig further into the passage, we read about the dew from Mount Hermon flowing onto Mount Zion. Mount Hermon was considered a sacred mountain, the mountain on the northern limits of the promised land. Mount Hermon produces significant amounts of dew, which is vastly different from Mount Zion, a drier mountain. The overflowing dew of Mount

---

2 Dooley, Jordan Lee. "Blog." Jordan Lee Dooley.com. https://jordanleedooley.com/blog/.

Hermon, of our unified relationship with sisters in Christ, flows onto the drier, less sacred, Mount Zion. This is how we impact the secular world around us: we allow the dew of our healthy Christian relationships to pour out onto the dry and barren souls we encounter.

Dwell in Unity: to live united, a complete and pleasing whole. This type of living among believers is considered to be like that of sweet perfume. Think about your favorite perfume, and I don't mean a Bath and Body Works spray, although I do enjoy a good Bath and Body Works spray. I personally love Chanel perfume; the scent is classic and feminine but not floral. For me, it's the perfect perfume. But that perfect perfume carries a hefty price tag, which means I use it with intentionality. I don't just spray it willy nilly and treat it with carelessness because I know its value. That's what is being referenced in this Psalm: something so beautifully sweet that we know its value and treat it with intentionality. This is the gift of an intentional Christian relationship.

As you finish out today, I encourage you to meditate on the beauty of Psalm 133. Let's pray about how we are living in unity with our sisters in Christ. Are we pursuing relationship? Are we intentional? Do we resolve conflict in a godly way, or do we bolt when things get gritty? Have we experienced a sweet perfume-like friendship? It's a holy and beautiful thing. Let's invite God into solidifying relationships that are holy anointed and pursue a life lived in unity.

READ > ANALYZE > APPLY

Read Psalm 133.

> Has God spoken to you this week as you have prayed for your friend(s)? What has God challenged you with this week?

> Take time to evaluate how you "friend." Does anything need tweaking? What can you do to intentionally pursue or invest in a friend?

Week 2

SACRIFICIAL LOVE

INTRODUCTION

This week we will be focusing our study on the relationship between David and Jonathan, a beautiful friendship in history that we can learn so much from. As we learn about covenant relationships with God and what sacrificial friendship can look like, let's pray about how we can translate this into our lives today.

VERSE

"... let us not love with words or tongue but with actions and truth." 1 John 3:18, **NIV**

CHALLENGE

Do I show sacrificial love to my friends? Do I love selflessly and in a Christlike manner? Am I a true friend like David and Jonathan? Pray on this and wrestle out any areas needing refinement. Even the best of us can improve in this area. What is one way you can pray for a friend today? Lift her in prayer to our heavenly Father; intercede on her behalf and ask God to bless her.

Week 2
Day One

Many years ago, I had just graduated college and found myself in a weird place. Friends from high school and college had moved to new places. Some were getting married, and some were even popping out babies at a young age. I was enjoying finding my place in corporate America and finding my footing as an adult. But I quickly realized that after too many nights at home, I was feeling extra lonely. The reality that once we graduate into adulthood, the makeup of our friendships changes overnight shocked me. It was new and surprisingly difficult.

At this same time in life, my brother was engaged, and his fiancé was in a similar life place, craving friendship in this new season of life. After doing Bible study together and praying, we both realized we wanted to pursue friendship with one another. From that day on, we made relationship with one another a priority. We were intentional. So often we see friendship portrayed in Hollywood as some beautifully connected thing; it appears to simply fall into place so perfectly made. While friendship is beautiful and can provide amazing connection, it takes effort; nothing simply falls into place. There will be people that we find chemistry with, but we still have to put in serious effort to find depth and beauty in that relationship.

To this day, I am still friends with my sister-in-law, and she is my most dear friend. We put in the effort, even when it was hard, awkward, and uncomfortable. Things didn't fall perfectly into place. We didn't always feel connected, and we still, all these years later, have moments where it's not pretty. But the depth of love and security felt in this friendship is a beautiful thing. I know that I can be all sorts of not pretty and have a toddler meltdown moment, and she will still love me and forgive me. Time and effort breed beautiful connection. Oftentimes, the most beautiful relationship comes from two people saying to each other, "This relationship matters to me." Rather than seeking out a kismet connection, we do the hard, awkward, and vulnerable.

We see this played out in the lives of David and Jonathan in 1 Samuel. These two men pursued friendship with great love and commitment to one another. As 1 Samuel 18 opens, David has just killed Goliath, and Jonathan's dad, King Saul, is very jealous of David. It wasn't exactly a friendship one would expect, and it definitely wasn't an easy one, given complexities of their relationship. But as we read, we see that Jonathan and David became one in spirit. In 1 Samuel 18:1, It even says that Jonathan loved David as himself. Wow. That's an amazing commitment to friendship.

Do you love anyone that much?

But this story shows us that life is rarely easy. To complicate matters, the Lord had chosen David to be the next king, and Saul was jealous. As a result, Saul kept David with him and didn't allow David to return home to his family. Even in all of the chaos and tumult, Jonathan and David remained friends. I don't know about you, but I would find it a little alarming to be best friends with someone my dad hated with such a jealous passion. (If there are any teen girls reading right now, please note that Saul's jealousy was evil and not of God... if your daddy doesn't like a friend, please listen to his wisdom.) But best of friends they were. Nothing, not Saul's jealousy and not David's successes, impacted the depth of their friendship.

These men made a covenant before the Lord because of their great love for one another. We read covenant and think agreement, but when this was written, a covenant was so much more. A covenant friendship meant that God was their witness; this was an agreement between them and God. Signed by the one and only Lord God, it's pretty darn sacred. This covenant involved a promise to one another: a promise to protect and love. This covenant was a change in relationship that was intended to impact generations to come.

Later in 2 Samuel 9, we see David take this literally. "Is there anyone left in the house of Saul to whom I can show kindness for Jonathan's sake?" (v.1, GW). And then we see the story of David and Mephibosheth unfold, a story filled with kindness and abundance for Jonathan's remaining family. Talk about friendship. I don't know about you, but this friendship sounds like the kind my heart hopes for.

As we continue to study David and Jonathan, we see the gift of friendship rooted in Christ and wholly committed to one another.

Read > Analyze > Apply

Read 1 Samuel 18–20.

> What in the story of David and Jonathan stands out to you?

> What heart issues are driving Saul's erratic behavior? How can you protect your heart from these same issues?

> Does your heart display Saul-like friendship or Jonathan-like friendship? In what way?

> Are there friendship traits in David's and Jonathan's relationship that you hope for in your friendships? If so, what are they? Take note of these; use them to pray over and process. If you have a friendship in mind that you desire this for, schedule time with that friend and share your heart's desires.

Week 2
Day Two

LEARN

> "...let us not love with words or tongue but with actions and truth." 1 John 3:18, NIV

CHALLENGE

This week we are praying for a friend as we evaluate how we love. Do I show sacrificial love to my friends? Do I love selflessly and in a Christlike manner? Am I a true friend like David and Jonathan? Pray on this and wrestle out any areas needing refinement. Even the best of us can improve in this area.

Friends, today we are going to dive back into 1 Samuel 18. Here we see this beautifully committed covenant friendship unfold. David goes out to kill Goliath and is abundantly successful. Based on Saul's reaction, it would be easy to assume that his son Jonathan would be jealous of David's success as well. With all that David did, he found more and more success and fame. But Jonathan wasn't jealous. Instead, Jonathan loved David for exactly who he was, with a love full of hope for his friend and with no malice in his heart.

This story should cause us as women to pause and ponder. We can love fiercely in all sorts of ways, but we tend to fall quickly into the realm of jealousy and envy. For whatever reason, it's a slippery slope for many of us stiletto-loving lipstick-wearing types. A heart that isn't pure towards a friend can easily be the death of a beautiful friendship. As we pursue relationship and find ourselves sliding towards jealousy, our immediate posture should be one of leaning into Christ and praying through it. God wants to lavish abundance on each of us in our own due time, but often when we are suffering greatly, our friends are succeeding in big ways. The true love of a friend celebrates the wins in a dear friend's life, lifting her to God in the most loving of ways, even when your life is crumbling to pieces.

Jonathan even gifted David his robe, tunic, sword, bow, and belt. I would love to offer you a beautiful analogy for what this type of gifting might look like in our world today, since I'm guessing you aren't running around in a robe and tunic with a bow and arrow strapped to your back, but there isn't one. Any gift given with selfless and abundant love is to be treasured. Many years ago, my husband was between jobs, and we were struggling to make ends meet. A friend from church received a hefty raise, and rather than use it on something fun for his family, he and his wife committed to paying our mortgage until employment was found. Have you ever been lavished with a love-filled gift like this? This selfless and sacrificial gift still stirs my soul with abundant gratitude. True friendship doesn't count the dollar cost; it desires the best for the receiver, end of story. And I believe wholeheartedly that God delights in this kind of giving, so much so that it will not return void.

Sit in this for a minute: Jonathan knew that God desired for David to be king. Do you think maybe Jonathan, the son of Saul, the current king, wanted to be king someday? I can't help but think he dreamed at times of being king; doesn't that seem logical for the son of the king? And now he is best friends with the man he knows will eventually be king, which means he will never be king. Jonathan desired God's will over his own human desires. We see a man wholly committed to his friend, a friendship he invited God into in a mighty way, despite his dad, the king, hating the man and despite that same man taking his place as future king. Even the humblest of people might struggle with this, but not Jonathan; he was delighted to be David's friend. This is how we "friend" well. This is how we commit to friendship that stands the test of time.

As I was preparing for this study, I studied the letters of Paul to the churches. I was curious to see what prayer for our brothers and sisters in Christ looked like. Many of Paul's letters include a prayer for them of grace and peace from Christ. He mentions it over 30 times! Our posture to our sisters in Christ should be that of praying God's grace and peace on them. What a beautiful way to love our friends and soften our hearts to all God desires for them. As we see in 1 Samuel, a friendship rooted in Christ is pure. It delights in the amazing person God created our friend to be, celebrating her unique strengths and abilities. A friendship rooted in Christ thanks God for how he made her and the beauty she brings to our lives. Imagine the shift in our hearts when our posture towards friendship is to pray blessing and abundance on those we love. It shifts the entire dynamic of the relationship to one that is about serving Christ and not self and to loving like Jesus and not the world.

READ > ANALYZE > APPLY

Read 1 Samuel 18 again.

> › As you re-read this chapter today, did anything new stand out to you?

> › God has given David favor, and Jonathan understands that. How do you think their heart posture with God has impacted their friendship?

> › David had God's favor and, because of that, great success. What benefit or value did David's friendship with Jonathan bring him?

> › What benefit or value do your friends bring you? What benefit or value do you bring your friends? Think of a friend or two and pray "grace and peace from Christ" and abundant blessing in their lives.

Week 2
Day Three

Learn

"... let us not love with words or tongue but with actions and truth." 1 John 3:18, NIV

Challenge

This week we are praying for a friend as we evaluate how we love. Do I show sacrificial love to my friends? Do I love selflessly and in a Christlike manner? Am I a true friend like David and Jonathan? Pray on this and wrestle out any areas needing refinement. Even the best of us can improve in this area.

As we read into 1 Samuel 19 and 20, we see the friendship of David and Jonathan being tested. Life just went from complicated to crazy difficult. Saul is now seething with jealous rage and wants David dead. He's throwing spears at David and hunting him down to kill him. Things have taken a drastic turn, and this is now about life and death. As Hollywood so eloquently portrays for us, when things become a matter of life and death, we see commitments break and promises broken. This is when survival is all that matters, and betrayal steps in, but that's not how this story plays out. Instead, we see Jonathan loyally protect his friend.

As we read in 1 Samuel 19:1, Saul told Jonathan and all his attendants to kill David. But Jonathan was very fond of David and warned him.

Defying the king, his father, and possibly putting his own life at risk, Jonathan warns David. Have you ever loved a friend as selflessly as Jonathan? I'm hopeful that you have never needed to protect a friend from death. But maybe your selfless act caused you to lose favor at work or among a group of people. Or maybe selfless love required you to change the way you live around a friend so as not to be a stumbling block to that person. There are countless ways to love in a risky and selfless way, many of them requiring us to take a stand against what might be the norm.

One of the greatest gifts of true friendship is the benefit that relationship brings when life gets hard. But to experience that benefit, we have to first invest and give to that relationship. Before Jonathan protected his friend, he and David built a friendship over time with a foundation in God. I cannot urge you enough to put in the time. Get vulnerable, pray purposefully, and find a person to invest in. I hope by now you are starting to see that true friendship is more about the other person and God than it is about you. If the foundation is there, and if we invest selflessly, the relationship can withstand trials.

Our family had a period of many years when my son was quite sick and constantly in the hospital. It was never a planned or known thing. One day something would happen, and it would be a rush to the emergency room and an inevitable hospital stay. During those years, we found ourselves between employment opportunities, and it felt like every single day we took a new hit. Those years were extremely difficult. We found, though, that it was the true test of friendship. When life got hard and we didn't have much to offer, that's when some of our friends left, and some of our friends that had the greatest opportunities to offer support didn't. Those that stayed and walked in the weeds with us were the biggest blessings.

I remember the girlfriend that every time I called on the way to the emergency room with my son, she would rush over to be with the other kids. Oftentimes my house was an absolute disaster, and she found little sleep. But every single time, she rushed to meet our needs. She stepped into my role the next morning, caring for my other kids and loving them through another day of uncertainty with mom, dad, and brother away. That is selfless friendship; that is love. And then again when I found myself in the hospital for some time, friends rotated nights so I wouldn't be alone, sacrificing sleep and comfort to step in and be there for a friend in need. This is the hope for friendship, and this is what selfless love looks like. But we don't get here overnight. We have to put in the time, knowing the reward is well worth the investment. Sometimes, even when we've invested, friendships don't last through the hardship. The ones standing with us when everything around us has been destroyed? Those are the blessings we hang onto for life, the friends that know and exude the sacrificial love of Christ.

READ > ANALYZE > APPLY

Read 1 Samuel 19–20.

› Does anything stand out to you? Is there something here that grabs your heart? How does Jonathan sacrificially love David in these chapters?

› What are the traits of Jonathan that you would consider relatable and relevant to how you friend?

› How sacrificial are you as a friend? Ponder and consider ways you could sacrificially love a friend right now.

Week 2
Day Four

LEARN

> *"... let us not love with words or tongue but with actions and truth."* 1 John 3:18, NIV

CHALLENGE

This week we are praying for a friend as we evaluate how we love. Do I show sacrificial love to my friends? Do I love selflessly and in a Christlike manner? Am I a true friend like David and Jonathan? Pray on this and wrestle out any areas needing refinement. Even the best of us can improve in this area.

A few years ago, our family relocated from the Midwest to the Carolinas. We had spent much of our life living in our lovely little Midwest town, which meant we were leaving a treasure trove of friendships. While you can stay friends from a distance, the harsh reality is that the friendships shift and look different. Proximity isn't everything, but it sure helps a friendship stay solid. I still maintain friends from our life before the move, and I love them fiercely, but the pain from leaving was intense. If I'm being brutally honest, there is still a sting from that separation. God was calling us to a new place for Him, and we willingly went, filled with excitement for all that was to come but heartbroken by all we had to leave.

As we encounter David and Jonathan in 1 Samuel 20, we see David needing to leave Jonathan to flee for his life. That has to be absolutely soul-crushing for these two friends, especially knowing they may never see each other again. There weren't cell phones for texting and calling or even emails for keeping up; this was going to be really "gone." I struggle to process that in light of the heartache I felt leaving friends that I can still call, text, or email when I want. I wonder if Jonathan might have questioned being honest with David about the Saul situation in hopes that he wouldn't need to flee? It's possible that dishonesty would have led to the death of David; talk about being bold by choosing to be honest with David.

As the chapter unfolds, we see Jonathan and David wrestle out their trust. Can you imagine this happening in real life?! It's like we are watching a Netflix drama play out in the Scriptures. These two men are trying to figure out how much danger David is in, and then they're trying to sort out their loyalty to one another amidst such uncertainty. In verse 17, we even see Jonathan reaffirm his oath to David because he loved David as himself. Then we see the plan and purposefulness in how the two protect one another, continually reiterating their commitment to one another through the Lord.

These two men had a sworn friendship before the Lord, and we see the chapter close out with David fleeing for his life. Jonathan had to share the harsh truth with David that his very own father intended to kill him. Talk about rough! But Jonathan doesn't sugarcoat the truth. He steps boldly into the uncomfortable and then works out a plan to help his friend. The more we pursue friendship, the more likely a day will come when we have to share or face an uncomfortable truth with a friend. We are broken and frail beings with sin nature. No matter how much God molds our lives to be like him, we may still need the wisdom and truth of a friend. But we see these men model how a God-filled friendship can step into the messiness of truth and still honor one another. They offer grace and love, and a solid commitment to the Lord and one another.

We read in 1 Samuel 20:23, *"...the Lord is a witness between you and me forever "(NIV).* That gives me chills. This is doing life together. This is the friendship we should all strive for: one that is openly vulnerable to one another and the Lord for our whole lives.

And then we see them weep together over the difficulty of the situation. David is needing to flee, and their hearts are broken. We offer abundant love when we weep with our friends who are weeping, mourn with our friends who are mourning, and rejoice with our friends who are rejoicing (Romans 12:15).

> *"Do not forsake your friend..." Proverbs 27:10 (NIV)*

Forsake means to abandon. We are best when we step into the uncomfortable with our friends to the depth of tears, abandoning our own selfish desires, and instead offering unconditional love and support. This is sworn friendship before the Lord, a promise of commitment to relationship before our God.

Read > Analyze > Apply

Read 1 Samuel 20.

> What is something you learned when reading this chapter?

> In verse 31, Saul mentions Jonathan's kingship is not secure with David alive. What do you think a normal response to that would be? What was Jonathan's response?

> How could you take David and Jonathan's story and apply that to your friendships today?

> Pray for your heart in relation to your friends. Ask God to show you specific friendships where you can love like David and Jonathan.

Week 2
Day Five

Learn

"...let us not love one another with words or tongue, but with actions and truth." 1 John 3:18

Challenge

This week we are praying for a friend as we evaluate how we love. Do I show sacrificial love to my friends? Do I love selflessly and in a Christlike manner? Am I a true friend like David and Jonathan? Pray on this and wrestle out any areas needing refinement. Even the best of us can improve in this area.

As we finish up our study on the friendship of David and Jonathan, we are impacted by this great example of true friendship. Outside of Jesus, there is no perfect friend, but these two are darn close. They show us the value of being intentional in our friendships, taking time to pursue friends and lift them in prayer to Christ. I urge you to consider praying "Grace and Peace to you from Christ" for your friends regularly. Let's commit to lifting friends we love to God in prayer regularly, praying the best for all God has in their lives.

As we pray for our friends, we often find our passion for them increasing, and our desire to see them succeed in all they do grows. Our heart leans into God's perfect plan for their lives, and their strengths are no longer a threat to us in any way. We are grateful that God gave them those gifts to serve Him. We want to see them excel in all they do, and our love becomes purer and less complicated. The strength of this love allows us to challenge and refine one another, helping mold us to be more like Christ. And this is where we start to see a massive

Kingdom impact in our friendship because now it's about something much bigger than her or me: it's about God.

> *"As iron sharpens iron, so one person sharpens another." Proverbs 27:17, NIV*

In prayer, we are reminded of the loyalty we feel for this beautiful friend. We become willing to jump into the messy, uncomfortable, and oftentimes inconvenient to support her in life. Once we've invested so many minutes, hours, and maybe even years into a relationship, let's not walk away when it gets uncomfortable but rather dive into the muck and help carry her through it. Let's support until it hurts and then maybe more. Let's love unconditionally, serve wholeheartedly, and encourage with all of our being. Jesus sacrificed for us; let's be willing to do the same for our friends. Sacrifice is the litmus test for a true friend. Let's be sure we are true friends.

Read > Analyze > Apply

Read 1 John 3:16, Mark 10:45, John 15:13, John 13:34, 1 Samuel 20:14–17 and 2 Samuel 9:7–11.

> Did anything about David and Jonathan's friendship challenge you? Pray consider next steps.

> Based on the verses we just read and the story of David and Jonathan we studied, what do you consider the pillars to a strong friendship?

> Take these pillars and rank how you currently friend in each category. Process how you could improve in each area.

> Dying happens one time, but living requires intentionality every single day. What are some intentional things you can do to strengthen your friendships?

Week 3

LOYALLY COMMITTED

INTRODUCTION

There is an abundance to be found in friendships that challenge us while encouraging us. This week we are going to dive into the benefit of friendship with our sisters of all ages, gleaning wisdom and insight as we digest the benefit of diversity in relationships. Whether you are older and wiser, younger and still learning, or somewhere in between, there is much to be gained from diversity of relationships and from friends that challenge us outside our normal (think comfort zone). I hope as this week's study unfolds you too grasp the beauty and benefit of older, younger, and everyone in between, journeying together as friends.

VERSE

"Above all, love each other deeply because love covers over a multitude of sins. Offer hospitality to one another without grumbling. Each of you should use whatever gift you have received to serve others, as faithful stewards of God's grace in its various forms. If anyone speaks, they should do so as one who speaks the very words of God. If anyone serves, they should do so with the strength God provides, so that in all things God may be praised through Jesus Christ. To him be the glory and the power for ever and ever. Amen." 1 Peter 4:8–11, NIV

CHALLENGE

Does your inner circle include wise friends? Are you a fair-weather friend, or do you help carry friends when adversity hits? Take time to pray and consider how you friend. This week I challenge you to encourage a friend who is struggling, maybe by taking her out to dinner, sending flowers or a care package, mailing her a handwritten note, or calling her and investing in focused time with just her. Whatever it should look like, encourage her.

Week 3
Day One

Friends, journey with me to a different time in my life, a time when my faith was shaken to its core, and I wasn't sure I could give another second of my life to God. I had lived year after year, month after month, day after day, and sometimes even minute after minute in absolute chaos. All my stability and security had been completely ripped to shreds, and there was nothing stable or secure anymore. The future appeared uncertain, and the recent past had become too difficult to stomach. My faith was at an impasse; I could either choose God and accept that this difficulty could be the rest of my days, or I could decide to accept defeat and walk away. My heart was breaking. No choice offered me certainty for my future, and I was sure that God had abandoned me, so walking away seemed the solution. But I couldn't give up on God. Not a God that I knew had to be there somewhere. Somewhere deep in my heart, there was still a longing for God in my life.

Not long after this decision, the decision to trust my unknown future to a God that I maybe kind of knew, my world was rocked even more. I clearly remember crying out to God "We were just here! Will it ever end?!" I was processing this with an older, wiser friend, one who had more faith years under her belt and had lived her fair share of "why" moments. She counseled me with words that, to this day, still shape my faith. I was sharing with her that it felt like once again the rug had been pulled out from under me, but that I finally got it: security was an illusion, and God is the only stable ground in life. That's when she told me that, "a blessed faith existence is one where life feels like one long and crazy roller coaster ride. This is when we know that God is shaping us in this journey called life. To be pursued like that is a priceless blessing." Her wise and encouraging words gave me the buoy I needed to trust God wholeheartedly despite unsteady life circumstances.

This wise woman, along with a few others, shaped my faith life through theirs. They modeled commitment to Christ, loyalty and respect in marriage, Christ-honoring friendship, how to love through trials, and what Christian community looks like. My days don't involve regular interactions with them any longer, but the impact on my life is still there. The investment they made in me when my faith was still young and growing, when I was newly married and when I was a young mom, are priceless.

As you inventory friendship in your life, have you ever had a friend that was either older or younger than you?

In Titus, Paul shares with us how older and younger women can support and encourage one another.

Read with me Titus 2:3–5.

Do these verses make you cringe? Or does the idea of friendship regardless of age excite you?

If you read these verses and felt your whole body stiffen in response, I get it. It leaves us feeling like someone else has carte blanche to tell us how to live life, and that doesn't sound fun. I don't know about you, but most days, I feel like I'm doing just fine and don't need anyone telling me my business; I mean it's MY business. Right?! But what if there is a biblical foundation for those older and younger celebrating their differences, leaning into their strengths and experiences, and walking arm in arm? I don't think Paul is pointing and waving his finger in a judging way; I think he is offering insight into the beauty of women of all ages in the church walking through life together. It is prudent to understand that not all women with a few more years of experience in life are wiser, just as women who are still younger might not be foolish. Age doesn't equal wisdom, but that's part of what Paul is touching on here. He is urging wise and holy living regardless of age and intentional connectedness of God's daughters.

I often imagine a National Geographic documentary when I hear older and younger referenced, one filled with women hiking miles with big jars to obtain water, sometimes with kids strapped to their bodies, and crouching in the river while they wash their clothes. And then the women huddle around a big village fire together, preparing and cooking dinner for their families. I imagine in this scenario, it's easy to learn from one another and do life together. I'm guessing the older mentoring the younger is a natural order of things, and likely those conversations are easy to have when doing so much of the same activities together day in and day out. We hear the phrase "it takes a village" and struggle to comprehend past this National Geographic picture. Right or wrong, society in America is very much isolated and not village-like. There might be some pockets of communities and families living more in sync and supporting one another, but that's rare. We are smack dab in the middle of "you do you" culture, and whether it be pride or not wanting to be a burden, we rarely ask for help. With this type of thinking and lifestyle, we cannot experience the true benefit of older and younger supporting and encouraging one another.

Many of our beautiful sisters in Christ have lived so much in their days, and those years of living offer perspective to others who haven't quite amassed the same experiences. If these sisters live in a way that is wholly committed to Christ, honoring Him with their days and spending their abundant free time investing in others, their Kingdom impact on the next generation has the potential to be exponential. When Paul was writing this to the people of Crete, women past their childbearing years were bored, so bored that they spent their days drinking wine and gossiping together. The women had lost purpose in life and subsequently spent their days frittering away their time. God never wants us wasting our time here on earth; He desires for us to boldly embrace Kingdom living no matter the season in life.

Have you ever met another woman and thought, "someday I want to be just like her?" What about her stood out to you? Was she passionate about something; extremely kind; selfless and giving abundantly to those around her; feisty and able to drive change for the better; or maybe it's something else entirely? Take a minute to ponder: who is the woman you want to become? If you aren't already, when you are old and gray, who do you want to be? If you are wiser in your years, are you the woman you always wanted to be?

Each of the special women who invested in my life had qualities that I admired and at least one trait I hope to one day master. There is so much benefit to being challenged by the life of a sister in Christ. Take a minute and think about someone in your life whom you admire. What about her is something you strive to emulate? Maybe this is a good time to reach out and schedule a coffee date with her.

READ > ANALYZE > APPLY

Read Titus 2:3–5.

› List the desired traits of women referenced in this passage.

› Do you feel you are an older or younger woman? Highlight the list of traits outlined above that apply to you.

› How can you take those highlighted items and apply them to your life? Are there any traits that could use improvement? Pray about your involvement with other women in the church.

› What is one thing you can do today to intentionally grow and improve as a Titus 2 woman?

Week 3
Day Two

Learn

> *"Above all, love each other deeply because love covers over a multitude of sins. Offer hospitality to one another without grumbling. Each of you should use whatever gift you have received to serve others, as faithful stewards of God's grace in its various forms. If anyone speaks, they should do so as one who speaks the very words of God. If anyone serves, they should do so with the strength God provides, so that in all things God may be praised through Jesus Christ. To him be the glory and the power for ever and ever. Amen." 1 Peter 4:8–11, NIV*

Challenge

Does your inner circle include wise friends? Are you a fair-weather friend, or do you help carry friends when adversity hits? Take time to pray and consider how you friend. This week I challenge you to encourage a friend who is struggling,; maybe by taking her out to dinner, sending flowers or a care package, mailing her a handwritten note, or calling her and investing in focused time with just her. Whatever it should look like, encourage her.

Join me as we dive into Ruth, the sweet little book of four chapters that feels almost like a rom-com playing out on the pages. But today we aren't here for the romance.

Go ahead and read Ruth chapter 1.

Has life ever left you tired? Like a deep down to the bones weary, the kind of tired that leaves you depleted straight through to the soul? I've been there before.

Sometimes life has this way of sucker-punching us left and right then leaving us with nothing left to give. As we open our time in Ruth today, this is where we find Naomi. She and her husband fled famine in Israel to Moab. They end up staying in Moab for many more years than anticipated, ten to be exact, and Naomi's husband dies during this time. Her sons marry Moabite women, and then her sons also die. We see lots of heartaches as we begin this journey with Ruth and Naomi.

There is a significant amount of biblical history with Moab; it's a pagan land that has historically been hostile to Israel. We are reading this story in the time of the Judges. So here we are in a pagan land, a land that doesn't love God, in a time when every man did what was right in his own eyes (Judges 21:25). Let that sink in…. every man did what was right in his own eyes. We now have two Moabite women, Ruth and Orpah, and their Israelite mother-in-law, all left widowed. At this particular time in history, a childless widow was among the lowest and most disadvantaged social classes. These women would have been completely dependent on the generosity of strangers for survival. This is also where we see Naomi realize that she needs to journey back to her hometown of Bethlehem.

I'm going to venture a guess that this wasn't an easy decision. She was leaving the place she had called home for many years and now heading back to her hometown in the lowest of lows. I imagine it carried the same dread as that of a high school reunion; she would have much preferred to arrive back home successful and prospering. Waltzing into town with two Moabite daughters-in-law and zero grandchildren isn't going to win her points; it would accomplish quite the opposite. But here we are in the story, ready to begin the long trek back to Bethlehem.

Somewhere towards the beginning of this journey, Naomi urges Ruth and Orpah to turn around and return home. Why Naomi has a change of heart we don't know; it could have been a truly selfless desire for these women to find a great life, or it could have been selfish in that she didn't want to arrive home with two pagan daughters-in-law. Regardless of Naomi's heart when prompting this, it would have seemed quite difficult, if not impossible, for Ruth and Orpah to find an Israelite husband. We see Orpah hug and cry and turn around for her home, filled with grief and heartache as she journeys back to her family. But Ruth? Ruth won't relent.

> *"…Don't urge me to leave you or to turn back from you. Where you go I will go, and where you stay I will stay. Your people will be my people and your God my God." Ruth 1:16, NIV*

At a time when every man did what was right in his own eyes, Ruth placed her loyalty and trust in Naomi and Naomi's God. This is radical. What do you think prompted Ruth to make such a bold, and from all appearances, unwise choice? Why Naomi? And why her God? Did Ruth have family that would be generous to care for her until she could remarry? Would her survival have been easier in Moab?

This was a big commitment, something much bigger than anything we can fathom or understand. God was in the details, and we see the beginning of a noble commitment of one to the other. Two women forced together through marriage now choose to walk the difficult unknowns of their future together. As we touched on earlier in our study, some of the most beautiful friendships are born out of commitment despite adversity. At this time in their story, these women had no idea what the future held; I would guess they didn't even fully comprehend the enormity of the decision made right here. But, at this moment, they made a committed choice and walked arm in arm through the journey ahead.

The trek from Moab to Bethlehem was about 50 miles. That seems like nothing to us; we hop in the car, and off we go, an hour of our day gone, and we are on to the next thing. But this was a journey on foot through rough terrain, an exhausting journey that would take about two full days to complete. I like to imagine the conversations they had on this two-day trek. I wonder if they shared about hopes and dreams, fun stories of their husbands, and childhood experiences, maybe along with their heartache and fear. I would guess that this journey to their next destination laid a solid relationship foundation, one that set them up for success in all that was to come. But make no mistake; they likely also found themselves tired and cranky, impatient that one needed to rest or take a drink when the other wanted to keep going, frustrated that she chews too loudly, or her shoes make noise, or she breathes with a whistle. You can bet that this journey had its not-so-pretty moments, but despite it all, they journeyed together.

One of the most beautiful gifts of friendship is journeying together through life. It sometimes offers rough terrain; it's never just laughs and fun, but the reward of a life lived with other women is priceless. Have you journeyed through adversity with a friend? What stands out to you about that journey together? Does any of that memory prompt you to pray for your friend or maybe send a text letting her know you appreciate her? Is there anything worth noting and remembering for the next time you and a friend encounter adversity? Use this time to pray and let God reveal His desires for friendship and relationship in your life.

READ > ANALYZE > APPLY

Read Ruth 1.

> What did Ruth promise Naomi in verses 16 and 17? Why do you think Ruth made these commitments?

> In verse 17, Ruth tells Naomi "your God will be my God." How do you think God factors into Ruth's decision and the rest of this story? Do you have any friendships or relationships where your commitment to God and the other person is this strong?

Read 1 John 3:16.

> Pray about your current friendships and ask God to reveal any that would benefit from a godly commitment to that relationship. Is there a tangible next step to pursuing a godly foundation in this friendship? I encourage you to pray for this friend and invite God into the foundation of that relationship.

Week 3
Day Three

Learn

"Above all, love each other deeply because love covers over a multitude of sins. Offer hospitality to one another without grumbling. Each of you should use whatever gift you have received to serve others, as faithful stewards of God's grace in its various forms. If anyone speaks, they should do so as one who speaks the very words of God. If anyone serves, they should do so with the strength God provides, so that in all things God may be praised through Jesus Christ. To him be the glory and the power for ever and ever. Amen." 1 Peter 4:8–11, NIV

Challenge

Does your inner circle include wise friends? Are you a fair-weather friend, or do you help carry friends when adversity hits? Take time to pray and consider how you friend. This week I challenge you to encourage a friend who is struggling, maybe by taking her out to dinner, sending flowers or a care package, mailing her a handwritten note, or calling her and investing in focused time with just her. Whatever it should look like, encourage her.

When I was a teenager, I had a friend that I shared the good news of Christ with. She eventually accepted Christ into her heart, and the trajectory of her life changed completely. I vividly remember her sharing with me about her conversion and the role I played in that process. Telling you this story, it's easy to assume that I was a Godly teenager exuding the love of Christ everywhere I went. While I was a Christian and spoke of the impact God had in my life, I was also struggling through teenager-like things and making some very poor choices. At that time,

I didn't feel like any part of my life screamed Christian; it was more of a "talk the talk" but don't "walk the walk" time in my life. While God was gracious to this friend and grabbed hold of her heart through me and despite me, there were just as many friends seeing me live a double life.

As we encounter Naomi in the beginning of Ruth, I think this is where her heart and life are. She knows and loves God, but she is living a double life of sorts. When things got hard, rather than stick it out with God, her family fled to a pagan land. When living in that pagan land, she encouraged (or allowed, however your brain processes that) her sons to marry pagan women. This is not what God told his people to do. We are seeing a woman who still has a love for her God but isn't wholly committed to life with Him. She is living outside of the safe boundaries God created for his people. And as life has taken her to a place of absolute devastation, we see her making the slow trek back to her people and God.

Until this point in the story, we have seen very little evidence of faith in Naomi's life.

> *"When Naomi heard in Moab that the Lord had come to the aid of his people by providing food for them, she and her daughters-in-law prepared to return home from there." Ruth 1:6, NIV*

Naomi heard that Lord had been good to his people, and since there was nothing left for her in Moab, home she went to her family and her God. How many of us have lived outside of the boundaries God desires for us, only truly finding our way back when we are gutted to the core? God will pursue us whether we are in a pagan land or in the seats of a church. If our hearts aren't wholly committed, He will lovingly pursue us in hopes we turn fully to Him.

But here is where this story gets fun. As Naomi and Ruth have been crushed through loss and are left with few options, they both turn to Naomi's God. Let me say that again... they BOTH turn to GOD. Despite what appears to be very little fruit of faith in Naomi's life, Ruth's heart knows she needs Naomi's God. God can work through us despite us, and God can use that work He is doing through us and despite us to tug our own hearts closer to Him. Even the littlest of faith can grow the mightiest of stories for His Kingdom (Matthew 17:20). Ruth and Naomi are part of a much bigger story in history, and Jesus Christ would be born through their lineage because of this decision to follow God.

The lineage.... Ruth and Boaz birthed Obed – Obed fathered Jesse – Jesse was David's daddy, plus 25 generations, continuing on to Joseph – and then Jesus Christ (Matthew 1).

Let's refresh our memory and read Ruth 1 again.

As Naomi finds her way into Bethlehem, it creates quite the stir. I mean, the woman was ten years older and had likely aged quite a bit; she was also very much heartbroken and grieving. I'm sure she appeared to be a hollow version of the Naomi who had left so many years ago. And I wonder if people thought maybe her whole family, including her, had died? As the story is written, it doesn't appear that the family intended to be gone for years upon years; it's quite possible that people had feared the worst for this family. Yet here is Naomi, and now she is asking to be called Mara. Rather than try to play up the past ten years as some amazing journey, Naomi was honest with those she encountered. She didn't offer an Instagram perfect highlight reel; she shared her heartache.

> *"...Call me Mara, because the Almighty has made my life very bitter. I went away full, but the Lord has brought me back empty..." Ruth 1:20–21, NIV*

When Naomi could have allowed the bitterness of her heartache to make her life bitter, she instead leaned into the God she had forgotten for so many years. She understood that He hadn't abandoned her, and she journeyed, literally and figuratively, home to God. And isn't it so awesome that she did! Because she leaned into God and was wise with what she knew of Him, her faith impacted Ruth and ultimately the destiny of Israel, Gentiles, you, and me! It's easy to read stories in the Bible and assume that these people knew they were part of some big grand story for all of history to read about, but these women didn't know that. They knew that their hearts were breaking, their sense of security was gone, and the future looked bleak and uncomfortable. Nothing about this story felt grand to them; to them, it felt like survival. But right there, in the middle of the heartache and clenching of fists to survive, God swoops in to not only meet their need but also lavish them with His kindness.

Make no mistake; even if your life today feels similar to that of Naomi's, one filled with heartache and distance from God, He is not done pursuing you. Just about the time you think your life matters to no one, you might see your tiniest sliver of faith impact the life of a friend around you. Although God would love nothing more than to have all of your heart because of His great love for you, God doesn't need all of you or me to move in mighty ways.

> *"A new command I give you: Love one another. As I have loved you, so you must love one another. By this everyone will know that you are my disciples, if you love one another." John 13:34–35, NIV*

READ › ANALYZE › APPLY

› Note anything from Ruth 1 that you want to study further or meditate on.

› Does your life have any areas that need to turn back to God? Pray on this; let God show you they ways in which surrendering to Him will strengthen your relationship with Him.

Read John 13:34–35.

› The love referenced in this passage is a love of choice, not one founded in feelings. Are you loving the world this way, choosing to love even when it's difficult? How is your

› faith impacting the women around you? Can they see the fruit of God in your life? Are you shining His glory?

› Pray over this with your heavenly daddy. Let your Abba Father comfort your heart, encourage you in whatever life is like today, and open your eyes to the women around you desperate to know your God. There is no greater love than sharing the gift of salvation with those around you.

Week 3
Day Four

Learn

"Above all, love each other deeply because love covers over a multitude of sins. Offer hospitality to one another without grumbling. Each of you should use whatever gift you have received to serve others, as faithful stewards of God's grace in its various forms. If anyone speaks, they should do so as one who speaks the very words of God. If anyone serves, they should do so with the strength God provides, so that in all things God may be praised through Jesus Christ. To him be the glory and the power for ever and ever. Amen." 1 Peter 4:8–11, NIV

Challenge

Does your inner circle include wise friends? Are you a fair-weather friend, or do you help carry friends when adversity hits? Take time to pray and consider how you friend. This week I challenge you to encourage a friend who is struggling, maybe by taking her out to dinner, sending flowers or a care package, mailing her a handwritten note, or calling her and investing in focused time with just her. Whatever it should look like, encourage her.

As we continue into chapter 2 of Ruth, we see Ruth meet Boaz. It's easy to see romance in this story... can't you imagine Meg Ryan playing Ruth as she heads to the fields trying to find grain for her starving family, the hard and loyal worker whose beauty is noticed by the noble landowner Boaz, likely played by Javier Bardem? It feels like the making of the perfect rom-com. Even though I love a good romance movie, today we are going to focus on other parts of this story.

Read Ruth 2.

In Ruth 2:4, we read that Boaz has just returned from Bethlehem. It's a tiny little verse that seems insignificant to the story, but that's far from the truth. Boaz's field is in a town next door to Bethlehem, two miles to the east. That day he happened to return from a visit to Bethlehem, where it's safe to assume he heard of Naomi's return and Ruth's kindness to Naomi. These are details that are paramount to all that unfolds in the rest of the story of Ruth. Let's take a minute to process how Ruth found Boaz's field.

We read,

> *"And Ruth the Moabite said to Naomi, 'Let me go to the fields and pick up the leftover grain behind anyone in whose eyes I find favor.' … As it turned out, she was working in a field belonging to Boaz, who was from the clan of Elimelek." Ruth 2:2–3, NIV*

She found herself working in Boaz's field. How do you think that happened?

I think it's easy to read this story and assume that Ruth went around the corner to a random barley field. But no, Boaz's field was two miles outside of Bethlehem. TWO MILES. Again, this is before cars and the modern conveniences of life, like google maps. (Anyone else need to fully rely on google maps? No? Just me?) Ruth probably had some idea of where to head, but I'm guessing she started her journey a little unsure of what was next, all while hoping to find a barley field where she might "find favor." She trekked two miles outside of Bethlehem to find a field in which to glean, and she happened to find herself in Boaz's field ON THE DAY that he returned from Bethlehem. This is not some easy to comprehend random occurrence. This is God moving in mighty ways!!

Sometimes in life, we see God move and we miss it, but in reality, God moved in robust and amazing ways. I promise this story has amazing God-sized details, and we want to pay close again so as not to miss them. God was in every single little detail of this story. He was working in Ruth's heart, and she leaned into His prompting; He was softening Naomi's heart, and she leaned into all He was doing. This story can, and should, cause us to pause and ponder how God is moving in our hearts.

Right before my 30th birthday, I found myself quite ill. What I thought was a nasty asthma attack was actually bacterial pneumonia, and the infection had grown significantly. I was suddenly in the ICU and then the hospital for a period of days; and after coming a little too close to ending my days here on earth, I was facing a lengthy recovery process. My husband had been unemployed for over a year and was ready to start a new contract position two days after my returning home from the hospital. We had a baby and a toddler who needed all of me, and I was in no position to care for them on my own.

For the next few months, our beloved family and church family stepped in to care for me and my children. Our new neighborhood, full of strangers to us, stepped in generously to feed us. I still have memories of strangers coming to the door with the most amazing meals and treats, all of it made with love for people they didn't know. It still stirs up intense emotion when I remember being cared for so well by people who didn't have to care about the problems of some random family down the street or a few blocks over. For many months following this, I would run into a cashier at the grocery store or a mom at the park, and they would talk about the "sick mom" (me) that they prayed for. This was before "going viral" was a thing, but God moved mightily and prompted hearts to love on us in all sorts of big ways. Years later, I can tell you that some of these precious people became dear family friends, but at the time, they were just random strangers. This community is one where God wrote a beautiful story with us smack dab in the middle of it. The impact of strangers caring for us solidified a love for that community that couldn't be tamed.

At this point in the story of Ruth, I think it would be easy to see Ruth buckling under the pressure and changes in her life. She'd lost her husband and is in a new and foreign land. She knows little of their customs and ways of doing life. She is a complete and total outsider, a Moabitess no less. I'm not sure any of us would judge her if she lay in bed all day crying about the current state of her life. But instead, she takes initiative to meet her needs and the needs of Naomi. If you recall, they are at this point completely dependent on the generosity of strangers. It's safe to assume they are hungry, stressed, and not living in the best of accommodations; life is still kicking them in the rear. Ruth's commitment to Naomi, her people, and her God is still fairly new. How many of us have given up on something we've committed to in those first weeks or months? New Year's resolutions anyone?!

But we don't see Ruth buckle under the pressure; instead, we see her set out to hike miles outside of town to fields that likely won't be safe for her (remember, this was the time of the Judges when every man did what was right in his own eyes, and she is a foreigner), hoping to find even just a few grains falling off the table so that she and Naomi can eat. She had to be tired, but rather than wait for Naomi to figure things out, she took initiative and stepped into the unknown. God was gracious to her. He led her straight to the field of Boaz, setting into motion an amazing little story for the ages.

Boaz offered abundant kindness and generosity to Ruth, a total stranger. We see Ruth's response to Boaz in verse 13,

> "...You have comforted me and spoken kindly to your
> servant, though I am not one of your servants." ESV

Ruth is a foreigner from a pagan land, and a childless widow at that; she isn't even an equal with Boaz's servant girls. Yet Boaz offers her protection in his field, food and drink, and more than just a few random grains. Ruth could have eaten her fill and then been a little lazy since she has been offered such kindness, but instead, she brings leftovers to Naomi and works hard to bring home as much grain as possible. We see Ruth being generous and proactive. God provided favor, and she shared that abundance with her dear friend Naomi (2:18). She wasn't stingy or selfish; she was humble and kind and hard-working. Ruth exemplified sacrificial love and blessed Naomi, even when Ruth's own life was on the brink.

Friends, there is so much wisdom in how Ruth stepped in to do and love, and we should take note. This is how we love the women in our circle and even those who aren't in our circle. We step in until it hurts, we give selflessly even when it means we might feel the loss, and we trust wholeheartedly that our God is in the details. We shower the women in our world with robust abundance. I encourage you to pray and love all sorts of big; this is how we build lifelong relationships with our sisters in Christ.

READ > ANALYZE > APPLY

Read Ruth 2.

> Does anything in this chapter stand out to you?

> In verses 11 and 12, we see Boaz commend Ruth's devotion and heart for God. How do we see Boaz's heart for God on display in this chapter? How can this translate to friendship?

> Do you love those around you in big ways? Is there a woman in your life right now that you could shower with abundance?

> Do you show sacrificial love to your friends? Who can you encourage this week with some big love?

Week 3
Day Five

LEARN

> *"Above all, love each other deeply because love covers over a multitude of sins. Offer hospitality to one another without grumbling. Each of you should use whatever gift you have received to serve others, as faithful stewards of God's grace in its various forms. If anyone speaks, they should do so as one who speaks the very words of God. If anyone serves, they should do so with the strength God provides, so that in all things God may be praised through Jesus Christ. To him be the glory and the power for ever and ever. Amen." 1 Peter 4:8–11, NIV*

CHALLENGE

Does your inner circle include wise friends? Are you a fair-weather friend, or do you help carry friends when adversity hits? Take time to pray and consider how you friend. This week I challenge you to encourage a friend who is struggling, maybe by taking her out to dinner, sending flowers or a care package, mailing her a handwritten note, or calling her and investing in focused time with just her. Whatever it should look like, encourage her.

Today we find ourselves halfway through Ruth, and the wedding is coming.

If you are married, do you remember the days leading up to your wedding? All of that preparation and stress for the biggest party of your life? We see Ruth and Naomi preparing for what is to come, but it's vastly different from that of modern-day weddings.

Read with me Ruth 3 and 4.

As we encounter the beginning of Chapter 3, Ruth has been working hard in Boaz's field until the wheat and barley harvest is finished. She has been living with Naomi, and now they are past the harvest, so they are once again faced with the challenge of how to make ends meet. We see Naomi processing that Ruth deserves better, knowing a husband is the best chance of that. Please don't go feminist on me here; this is the culture and the best way for Ruth to find long-term safety and security.

But let's backtrack for just a second… Ruth and Naomi have been living together. Have you ever lived with a friend? At times it can be so much fun, and other times it is so dang challenging. These women are struggling through some super hard times and living together; you can bet there were some really ugly moments there. When we are tired and stressed and struggling to get through the days, the worst of us has a way of seeping through the cracks. I don't bring attention to this because we want to focus on the negative in this story but rather because it shapes the lens for what happens next.

Naomi is of the age that remarrying is out of the question, but that doesn't stop her from seeking marriage for Ruth. The Hebrew translation for "rest" here also means security (Ruth 3:1). Naomi knows that Ruth will find security, rest, and the best chance at a quality life with a husband. Let's remember that Ruth is a Moabitess, a foreigner, and the Israelites vehemently dislike Moab. Ruth is also a childless widow, which severely diminishes her desirability. Even if Naomi and Ruth can find someone who might consider marrying Ruth, he would likely not be a cream-of-the-crop, stand-up guy. But we serve a big God who wanted more for these women.

Do you feel like God wants the best for you, even when it looks like all hope is lost? God is in the business of taking broken, hopeless heaps and making beautiful masterpieces. In the middle of the broken, it often looks and feels like there is no hope and that the current state of ruins is "always and forever." I'm sure Ruth and Naomi questioned if there was any hope for their future, maybe even questioned God, but their story wasn't over yet. It's here that we see Naomi start to fight for her friend. In doing so, I like to think she prayed for Ruth, maybe even prayers of "more" for her friend; but regardless of what she prayed, we know she rolled up her sleeves and got busy helping Ruth. It's here we see Naomi start to fight for her friend. A kinsman redeemer, or **goel**, is hard for us to understand in today's culture, but this was considered proper at the time when it was written. Kinsman here means special family representative or chieftain. The role of the Kinsman Redeemer was to buy a fellow Israelite out of slavery; be the "avenger of blood" for a murdered family member, ensuring someone answers for the crime; buy back family land that has been forfeited; and carry on the family name by marrying a childless widow. While it was a right of Ruth's to pursue this, there were complexities that could have caused this to not go well. We see Naomi step in to instruct her friend. This is so valuable for many reasons, a big one being that Ruth is a foreigner and understands little of Israelite customs.

I have to laugh that Naomi instructs Ruth to clean up, perfume herself, and wear her best clothes. There is always wisdom in prettying up a little before pursuing a man, right?! A little perfume and a cute outfit never hurt anyone. Then we see Naomi advise Ruth to wait until Boaz goes to bed, and then she should uncover his feet and lay down. Awkward! This had to feel uncomfortable for Ruth, and I'm guessing outside of normal customs in Moab. Every single thing that Ruth is being told to do requires vulnerability on her part and an extreme trust in the wisdom and instruction of her friend. Because both Ruth and Naomi have been selfless in their love and friendship up to this point, Ruth can trust Naomi. Ruth trusted her friend that journeying out at night and sneaking into the bedroom of a man would be ok… that's a lot of trust!

Ruth told Naomi, **"I will do everything you say,"** (Ruth 3:5, CSB). And we see how a foreigner from a pagan land becomes married to a wealthy Israelite in the lineage of Jesus Christ. The translation describing Boaz as a mighty man of wealth also means "mighty man of valor." Ruth should never have ended up with such a wonderful man as her husband, but she did. And Naomi was blessed with a sweet grandchild to love. Isn't our God so amazing! Let's not overlook God's kindness and abundant blessing in all of the little and big details of this story.

In this story Boaz called Ruth a **"hayil"** woman, which translates to a woman of moral strength, quality, integrity, and virtue, the female equivalent to a mighty man of valor. This is what a life redeemed by God looks like. We go from foreigners in a pagan land to women of virtue in God's Kingdom. Naomi and Ruth supported, encouraged, and carried one another as they both found their way to God. As sisters in Christ, we have the privilege of walking life together in the same way. We can learn from one another, selflessly serve, and help our friends find rest and security in the hands of our mighty God. Regardless of age, we each have so much to offer our sisters in Christ.

READ > ANALYZE > APPLY

Read with me Ruth 3 and 4.

› Note all that God helped orchestrate in these chapters. Does this encourage you in your life today?

› In verse 14, the Israelite women speak to Naomi. Do you remember Naomi's interaction with the women in Ruth 1:19–21? What has changed?

› How can you love like Ruth and Naomi? Do you see value in investing in friendships of all ages? What is your favorite part of this Ruth story? Have you seen God work in mighty ways in your life, similar to that in the story of Ruth? What takeaways does this story offer us in light of friendship?

Week 4

FRIENDSHIP PILLARS

INTRODUCTION

This week we will be focusing our time on specific themes of friendship, evaluating how the Bible addresses each theme and how we can best strengthen our friendships in these areas. We will be looking at Kingdom, grace, encouragement, love + prayer, and servant heart.

VERSE

> "...if you have any encouragement from being united with Christ, if any comfort from his love, if any common sharing in the Spirit, if any tenderness and compassion, then make my joy complete by being like-minded, having the same love, being one in spirit and of one mind. Do nothing out of selfish ambition or vain conceit. Rather, in humility value others above yourselves, not looking to your own interests but each of you to the interests of others." Philippians 2:1–4, **NIV**

CHALLENGE

As we pour into themes of friendship this week {Kingdom, grace, encouragement, love + prayer, and servant heart}, let's pray about how well we rank in each theme. Are there any that you think you do well? Any that you could improve upon? Are there any tangible or practical next steps for those benefiting from improvement? If so, spend some time moving forward with those steps and enhancing the way you love and friend.

Week 4
Day One

LEARN

> "...if you have any encouragement from being united with Christ, if any comfort from his love, if any common sharing in the Spirit, if any tenderness and compassion, then make my joy complete by being like-minded, having the same love, being one in spirit and of one mind. Do nothing out of selfish ambition or vain conceit. Rather, in humility value other above yourselves, not looking to your own interests but each of you to the interests of others." Philippians 2:1–4, NIV

CHALLENGE

As we pour into themes of friendship this week {Kingdom, grace, encouragement, love + prayer, and servant heart}, let's pray about how well we rank in each theme. Are there any that you think you do well? Any that you could improve upon? Are there any tangible or practical next steps for those benefiting from improvement? If so, spend some time moving forward with those steps and enhancing the way you love and friend.

| KINGDOM |

My life these days is pretty darn frenetic. I spend my days juggling the demands of so many different things, and oftentimes it leaves me a little fuzzy and foggy. When I'm not able to focus on one thing, I sometimes find myself easily distracted and unable to complete anything. Add to that the phone in my hand almost 24/7, and my brain is a never-ending tilt-a-whirl!

We live in a world today that has an abundance of noise... streaming, Tik Tok, YouTube, Instagram, Facebook, never-ending ads, texts, and emails... there is no shortage of stuff. It's not uncommon for me to go to my phone to do something, but when I unlock it, I notice something else and deal with that, and then I see the next thing that pops up; before you know it, I've forgotten why I unlocked my phone. Instead, I spent time I didn't plan, on something(s) other than intended. Surely you can relate?! As I've been writing this study, I have found my brain all over the place.

One minute I'm looking up a verse or question, and then an ad pops up that grabs my attention, so I find myself window shopping for things I don't need. Then I get back on track, only to receive a text that I need to reply to, and then I remember an email I forgot to respond to, and I'm off track again. There is so much demand for our attention that it's easy to lose track of our priorities.

I took a paddleboarding class years ago, eager to learn the ways of the oh-so-popular activity. At the time, the closest body of water was a neighborhood pond; despite being cared for well, it was murky-looking and built over a quarry, so there were some crazy deep areas of the pond. I knew that I would likely take a tumble or two into the water during the class, but I was determined to do my best not to. After basic instruction, we were to get on our paddleboards and practice: practice how to stand, practice how to move forward and backward, practice circles, and practice leg placement for balance.

I never did fall during that class, but I spent that hour-plus insanely focused on the task at hand, paddleboarding successfully. I have gone out since and been less steady than that very first time because the more comfortable I get on the paddleboard, the less focused I become on my form and foundation. Kingdom living can be so very similar... we start out focused on Christ and the foundation He wants us to build, but as we "Christian" longer and life seeps in, we find ourselves less focused on heaven. This can quickly drown even the strongest of Christians.

Today, let's jump into Daniel 1 through 3.

Here we read about Daniel, Shadrach, Meshach, and Abednego, the noble young Jews who are handsome, smart, capable of working in Nebuchadnezzar's palace, and descend from Jewish royalty. Their homeland of Judah was "handed over" to King Nebuchadnezzar, and they were selected for special training in the palace of the King. They were to learn the Chaldean language and literature for three years, and then they would attend, or serve, the king. Almost immediately in Daniel 1, we read about God's provision for these young men. It says that God gave these men all they needed, He granted them kindness and compassion through the eunuch, and when the time came for them to go before Nebuchadnezzar, no one was found equal. And just like that, three years are completed in chapter one.

During those years, these men likely forged a strong bond and friendship. They were taken from their homes and families to a foreign land with foreign gods. While they were living in the palace and being trained for service to the king, I'm guessing they were missing their homes and former lives. Being the only Jews around, it's safe to assume they felt a strong bond and connection to one another. They were foreigners in a pagan land being taught the language of foreigners so they could serve a foreign king.

If you let that sink in for a minute, you realize they likely couldn't communicate with the other men and palace people for some time. I wonder if they had some knowledge of Babylon's customs or if it was all new. Since this isn't a time when the internet made knowing things easy, it's possible everything about their new home was foreign to them. That had to be extremely scary, overwhelming, and challenging. But when all of this went down, there were four Jewish men in this palace, and they could understand each other. Their customs, upbringing, language, and God were all the same.

Living in an ever-growing transplant area, I am constantly meeting new people who left their home state to venture to the Carolinas. When chatting, you can see the love of the place they relocated from. They share favorite restaurants, a special treat only found there, or maybe unique and fun festivals or events. There are specific things they miss about home, and amid a normal conversation, these little bits of love seep through. Whenever I run into someone from my home state, I almost squeal like a schoolgirl I am so excited. We chat about where in the state we lived, the State Fair, Casey's, Maid Rite's, snow, and so much more. It's an immediate connection to have known and loved similar memories and places. It's almost instant friendship, even if we have nothing in common except the state.

This is where we find these Jewish men, forging an instant bond and connection over something only they know and understand. Nothing draws us closer to others than our similarities; add in some adversity, and this is where lifelong bonds form. Do you think they laughed and joked about their lives back home? Do you think at times they were emotional or maybe even cried, missing their families? Do you think they were supporting one another in this new and challenging palace life?

Do you think it would have been easy for them to accept this as their new home and adapt to the ways of Babylon? Have you ever moved somewhere new and adapted to something specific to that area? We moved from the Midwest, where phrases like "ope" and "jeez" are commonplace, to the south where it's "y'all" and "fixing to." I'm not gonna lie; "y'all" has become a fairly regular part of my vernacular, and I realize this in no way impacts my salvation or eternity in heaven, but I think it does give an accurate representation of human nature. It's easy to acclimate to something new without even realizing we are doing so. But in this story, we see these men choose God. They knew that God wanted them to eat a diet different from the rest, and they fought the norm to continue to do so. We also see their faithfulness was rewarded with wisdom, knowledge, and success.

But man, Nebuchadnezzar is all sorts of crazy, and one day he was in such a mood. He wanted a scary dream interpreted. He hadn't been sleeping, and it was making him even more volatile than normal. None of the wise men would attempt to help because Nebuchadnezzar wanted them to tell him what his dream was, not just what it meant. He threatened to rip them limb to limb if they were wrong. Reading this, I really don't like this king… talk about insanity unleashed. But this is where the story leads, and because no one would interpret this dream, all the wise men were to be killed. But then Daniel bravely goes before the king to ask for time to interpret the dream.

Would you go before this insane ruler asking for permission to come back and potentially be torn limb to limb?! I don't think I would. I think I would be trying to hide from his men coming to kill me. But Daniel is a Godly man, and when granted his request, he immediately goes to his friends to pray.

When life gets upside down, do you immediately go to your friends to pray? It can be easy to overlook the power of prayer, to lose sight of our true King, but these men are amazing examples. Daniel and his friends Shadrach, Meshach, and Abednego prayed. God granted Daniel the words he needed to interpret the king's dream. And then what does Daniel do? He PRAISES. Y'all, when God comes through and answers prayer or meets needs, our immediate posture should be that of praise. Daniel gets it! And being a true friend, he promotes his friends to manage Babylon, but Daniel stays in the king's court. This little detail matters for the story to come.

For a while, we have business as usual, and then King Nebuchadnezzar once again finds himself in a mood. Aren't you so glad you never had to know this guy! He wants people to bow down to his 90-foot-high and 9-foot-wide gold statue every single time they hear his special music. Really?! Who needs a gold statue that is so monstrous? He has clearly forgotten his revelation that Daniel's "…God is the God of gods, Lord of kings and a revealer of mysteries…" (Daniel 2:47, NIV). But this is the king's current mood in all its crazy. And in the middle of all this, we find some jealous peeps who maliciously accuse the Jews of not bowing down, so now Nebuchadnezzar wants them to bow down or be thrown in the fire. Well… they don't bow down. I don't know about you, but if this were me, I would claim to be all brave and noble if this moment came, but I truly don't know if I would be. This is a fire that is seven times that of a normal fire, although our Jewish friends don't know this yet, and they have a decision to make. This fire killed all the men throwing them in it. All sorts of yuck. But ALL three of them refuse to bow down. All three!

How easy would it be to bow down and save your life? Don't we, solid and stable Christians, cave like that on the regular? How often do we shy away, thinking "I don't really have to say anything," or "this one time doesn't matter?" But these men faced certain death and STOOD THEIR GROUND. They loved GOD that much!!

Do you think it was easier to stand their ground since they were together? Do you think if it were just one of them, maybe it would have been easier to cave to the king's demands? Is there something to be learned from this? How do you think this represents Kingdom living?

When life is theoretically "throwing us in the fire," the people we surround ourselves with matter. Our friends matter! Are they pointing us heavenward, reminding us that God is on the throne, so we can do this? Or are they letting us off the hook? If we don't have them yet, I hope we strive toward Kingdom-focused friendships. The kind of friends who, when we get a little too comfortable on the paddleboard and are about to lose our balance, remind us that with our feet planted firmly in the right position, we can stand tall.

These three men went on to survive the fiery furnace, taking a haughty and foolish king to the feet of the One True God. And in the process of trusting God to rescue them from Nebuchadnezzar's wrath, they said "...even if he does not," we will remain faithful (Daniel 3:16, NIV). With the right people by our side, we can stand the heat and walk in the fiery unknown with our amazing Heavenly Father. Who we allow to speak into our lives matters immensely. The people we invite into our world should be doing everything in their power to face us heavenward, helping to carry us when the flames are too hot, and standing firm with us when it's a matter of life and death. We are God's Warrior Princesses, and a title of anything less is unacceptable. Tighten up that armor and stand firm! And choose wisely, ladies, because the people by our side truly make all the difference.

READ > ANALYZE > APPLY

Read Daniel 1–3.

› Did anything stand out to you from these chapters? Maybe something you've never noticed before? I know a couple of new "aha" moments came to me.

› When thinking of Kingdom focus in friendship, what verse or verses stand out to you? Note them in the margin.

› What are the key takeaways from each verse noted? How can those verses translate to your current life and friendships?

› Ponder and pray. Do you have wise and Godly friends in your inner circle? What do you think Kingdom-focused friendship looks like? Do you challenge your friends to lean on Christ when the flames start to burn? How can you strengthen your friendships to be fireproof?

Week 4
Day Two

LEARN

> "...if you have any encouragement from being united with Christ, if any comfort from his love, if any common sharing in the Spirit, if any tenderness and compassion, then make my joy complete by being like-minded, having the same love, being one in spirit and of one mind. Do nothing out of selfish ambition or vain conceit. Rather, in humility value others above yourselves, not looking to your own interests but each of you to the interests of others." Philippians 2:1–4, NIV

CHALLENGE

As we pour into themes of friendship this week {Kingdom, grace, encouragement, love + prayer, and servant heart}, let's pray about how well we rank in each theme. Are there any that you think you do well? Any that you could improve upon? Are there any tangible or practical next steps for those benefiting from improvement? If so, spend some time moving forward with those steps and enhancing the way you love and friend.

| GRACE |

Today I'm excited to chat grace with you ladies. Have you ever experienced an unexpected and immensely appreciated moment of grace? I remember being newly married when my husband, Ryan, and I took a tropical trip. As we were shopping on the trip, we stopped at a sunglasses store where I found the most amazing pair of designer sunglasses. I've always had a love of pretty things, and at that moment, these were one of my favorite pretty things. But we aren't fancy or uber-wealthy people, so the hubs did the prudent thing and put the kibosh on bringing those beauties home.

If you know me, you know that I don't give up easily. Upon our return home, I started looking for this pair of sunnies discounted. Love (or something like that) is love, right? I stumbled onto an eBay listing that had them majorly discounted, so I typed in a bid that I knew we could afford, all the while assuming there was no way I would win for such a low dollar amount. Imagine my surprise when the email arrived letting me know that I had won! But for some reason, the balance due was more than double the amount I had bid. I had overlooked one small, yet big, detail. I was bidding in another currency, and the conversion rate was over double what I had promised to pay! Uh oh!!

Ryan and I look back on this moment and laugh, but at the time it was less than funny. While he was pretty frustrated with me, and rightly so, I remember him treating me with grace. He didn't talk down to me or make me feel inferior, even though I missed a huge detail (math is not a strength of mine). It was by no means a stellar moment in our marriage from my side, but he exemplified grace, love, and compassion.

To experience grace in our lives, we must first mess up, which is no fun. Today we are going to dig into a Bible story that is full of no fun as we read Genesis 42 through 45.

Here we have the story of Joseph, a story that many of us are probably quite familiar with. As you may recall, Joseph's brothers are jealous of him and sell him into slavery. He ends up a slave to Potiphar, an officer of Pharaoh and captain of the guard. In Genesis 37, we read that Joseph was successful in serving his Egyptian master because the Lord was with him and made him successful. But like with any truly good drama, Potiphar's wife thinks Joseph is hot stuff. She propositions him multiple times, and he continually rejects her; as a woman scorned, she falsely accuses him of attacking her. This lands him in the king's prison. This poor guy can't seem to get a break. But the Lord is still with him, and he finds favor with the prison warden. So much favor, in fact, that Joseph is put in charge of the prison.

After Joseph has been in custody for a while, the king's cupbearer and baker are imprisoned. Both men have dreams that leave them visibly upset, so Joseph steps in to help, letting these men know that he's able to help because of his great God. He interprets accurately, and the cupbearer is invited back into the service of the king while the baker is hanged. Joseph asks the cupbearer to remember him if all goes well and to show him kindness by mentioning him to Pharoah. But the cupbearer forgets Joseph. Joseph cannot seem to catch a break.

Two full years pass, two years more years that Joseph has been in prison for no fault of his own. Pharaoh has a troubling dream, and suddenly the cupbearer remembers his prison mate Joseph. Joseph is summoned to the side of the king to interpret this dream. He is removed from the dungeon he has been living in—this is the exact word found in scripture, dungeon—and given clean clothes and a shave. I'll venture a wild guess that the king's dungeon isn't a place where one is able to live comfortably or cleanly.

Here Joseph lets Pharaoh know that, with the help of God, he can interpret the dream. And he does…. The people of Egypt will experience seven years of abundance and then seven years of famine. Joseph then advises Pharoah on next steps to ensure the best for Pharoah's people. Pharoah surprisingly says that there is no one in his Kingdom as discerning or wise as Joseph. This dude literally just came out of the dungeon and is now put in charge of this initiative to store up food and save the people. He is promoted to second to the king and given a signet ring, fine garments, and a gold chain. He was even given the second of the king's chariots and drivers that yell "Make Way!" for Joseph. Talk about a promotion; leave it to God!

Joseph has the Lord on his side and successfully implements the massive undertaking of storing up food for when famine strikes, so much so that they stopped measuring the stored grain because it was "beyond measure" (Genesis 41:29). The famine has now made it to Canaan, and Jacob (Joseph's dad) sends his sons to acquire grain in Egypt. This is where we catch up to today's reading and see the story of Joseph reuniting with his family unfold.

Read Genesis 42 through 45.

As we see Joseph test his brothers, it's like we can feel the heartache pouring out of the page. Joseph is overcome with emotion and weeps many times in these chapters. It had to be such a surreal experience to see his brothers unexpectedly show up; I would guess a whole slew of emotions came exploding to the surface. The anger of being wronged by them, the ensuing years of suffering and pain they caused, the love for his blood family, the curiosity about his dad, the sting of abandonment and rejection, and his heart's cry to belong with them again… I can't imagine any part of this story that didn't prompt extreme heartache and emotion reaching to Joseph's core. And as this unfolds, we see the brothers sort through similar emotions, the feelings of fear, guilt, love, and heartache. One mistake years ago has influenced the entire trajectory of this family's story. We know the ultimate outcome of this story is wholly for the glory of God, but I don't think it felt quite so God-ordained to them. Rather, it probably felt like repeated, utter defeat. We even read that Jacob cries out "Everything is against me!" (Genesis 42:36). Make no mistake; sin patterns and poor choices on the part of Jacob played into how this story unfolds, but this story is no doubt an intended part of God's plan, heartache and all.

As Joseph starts to see that his brothers have changed and are no longer the jealous ones he knew years ago, he invites them to his home to eat. He has his staff slaughter and prepare an animal, and he provides water to wash their feet and food for their donkeys. This is not the normal preparation for people who have wronged you. Do you think you would have been this generous if you were Joseph? Have you ever had to forgive and offer grace for a massive wrong done to you? It's far from easy to offer grace and mercy to those who have harmed us, whether intentionally or not. But that's exactly what Joseph does.

The remainder of this story is so beautiful. Joseph reveals his true identity and tells his brothers not to be distressed or angry with themselves (Genesis 45:5). Before these brothers have even had a chance to fully process what Joseph is saying, he is offering them forgiveness. I wonder how many lives would change if our immediate posture when wronged was to take it Christ and then offer the same grace He offered us. There is no greater freedom than forgiving and inviting God to handle justice, allowing our hearts to stay pure and reliant on Him.

What about Joseph do you think looked so different that the brothers weren't able to recognize him? Do you think God closed their eyes to recognition? Or maybe the older, wiser Joseph, who is now Egyptian, really looked that different?

What do you think is the most admirable trait in Joseph? Do you think that his years of suffering strengthened his relationship with God? Does suffering cause you to look heavenward?

Joseph saw God's fingerprints in his story, and he knew it was God's way of preserving his family. As we end chapter 45, Pharoah invites all of Joseph's family to Egypt and offers them the best of his land. The family is reunited, and Jacob has his sons all together again. These brothers would eventually become the heads of the Twelve Tribes of Israel. There is plenty of Biblical significance to this, but ultimately these twelve tribes enter the promised land and become the nation of Israel.

Joseph's wholehearted reliance on God molded him into a wise and holy man. When he had the opportunity to pay back evil for evil, he chose grace and mercy. Another way to explain grace is **unmerited mercy**. Mercy is **compassion or forgiveness shown toward someone whom it is within one's power to punish or harm**. Ultimately, it is forgiveness. The greatest gift we can bring to our friendships is grace. We will all screw up, forget important things, say mean words, and wrong our friends. I wish I could say to offer grace *if* a friend screws up, but this isn't an "if" kind of scenario. It is sure to happen; it's a question of **when** we screw up, not *if*. The beauty of friendship with a foundation in Christ is the forgiveness and grace that come from knowing and understanding that God offered us the ultimate forgiveness and grace.

READ > ANALYZE > APPLY

Read Genesis 42–45.

> Did anything in today's reading stand out to you?

> Where did you see grace applied in these chapters? Note it here. How do you think Joseph was able to offer so much grace so often?

> As we apply this story to friendship or relationship, what stands out to you? Is there a circumstance from now, or some time ago, where we should offer grace? I believe that by taking our hurts to God in prayer, we are offered insight into the heart of our perfect heavenly Father. Pray through this and lean into the wisdom God is offering.

Week 4
Day Three

Learn

> *"...if you have any encouragement from being united with Christ, if any comfort from his love, if any common sharing in the Spirit, if any tenderness and compassion, then make my joy complete by being like-minded, having the same love, being one in spirit and of one mind. Do nothing out of selfish ambition or vain conceit. Rather, in humility value others above yourselves, not looking to your own interests but each of you to the interests of others." Philippians 2:1–4, NIV*

Challenge

As we pour into themes of friendship this week {Kingdom, grace, encouragement, love + prayer, and servant heart}, let's pray about how well we rank in each theme. Are there any that you think you do well? Any that you could improve upon? Are there any tangible or practical next steps for those benefiting from improvement? If so, spend some time moving forward with those steps and enhancing the way you love and friend.

| ENCOURAGEMENT |

Today let's imagine we have just clicked play on the latest popular movie. The picture scrolls across the television. We see people viciously attacking a field and stealing all of the donkeys and oxen that were grazing, killing the workers, and fleeing. The next scene is one of fire consuming a pasture filled with thousands of sheep and goats and their keepers, everything dead and destroyed by the fire. And then there's a scene of people gruesomely attacking the handlers for a stable filled with thousands of camels, killing the workers and stealing every single camel. The camera pans to a house with seven brothers and three sisters inside, laughing and enjoying dinner together when suddenly a hurricane-like wind blows through and crushes the siblings under the wind-toppled house, all of them dead.

What horrific devastation. This is where we are going to start today, smack dab in the mess and chaos of Job.

Read Job 1 through 2 and 42 with me.

This story is such a hard one to read. We see a thriving and successful man who is wholly committed to God. "No one else on earth is like him, a man of perfect integrity, who fears God and turns away from evil" (Job 1:8, HCSB). And then in one fell swoop, he loses everything, including his children. This is a hard one to swallow, and it's easy to see our own reflection in the fear these passages can bring. But there is beauty as we see Job wrestle out his misfortune with God.

Have you ever wrestled out misfortune with God? While it's an extremely painful and gut-wrenching place to be, there is nothing that strengthens our faith more. It amplifies our need for God with every ounce of our being and clarifies the reality that we are left with only two choices: lean in and work it out with God or walk away. This is where faith that stands the test of time is born.

As we enter chapter two of Job, we see that Job's friends meet together to sympathize and comfort him. When they round the corner and see Job, they barely recognize him. The poor man was covered in boils from head to toe and in immense pain. He was laying in ashes as was customary to express grief and mourning. This man has lost everything including his health. His friends mourn with him as they weep aloud for their dear friend. They tore their robes to show their grief and sat with him in the ash.

For seven days and nights, his friends stayed there with him, not speaking because his pain and suffering was so intense. For seven whole days, they just quietly sat with a friend they cared for, feeling the turmoil and pain and heartache he was enduring. They were supportive and loyal and all that one can hope for in good friends. But then Job starts to speak, and the words out of his mouth are angry as he curses his life. For THIRTY-FIVE more chapters in this book, Job and his friends are talking. It starts out calm, each trying to communicate their thoughts, but by the end, they are full-on fighting. His friends are saying things like, "If I were you, I would appeal to God and present my case to him." They thought he had done wrong to deserve his circumstances and that he needed to atone for his wrongdoing. Job calls his friends "miserable comforters" (Job 16:2) and wonders how long they will continue to "torment him with words" (Job 19:2) as things continue to spiral out of control.

Have you ever found yourself in conflict with friends when your life is suffering?

I remember when someone I loved very dearly lost someone she loved immensely. The heartache was crushing, and the grief all-consuming. I rushed to her side and was there in the hospital and the moments and days after, but eventually, life returns to some semblance of normal. At least it did for me. I was back to juggling school drop-offs, work and nonprofit commitments, and the day-to-day glamour of cooking and cleaning. But for my friend, her world was and still is forever changed. The journey with her had some bumpy moments, some originating with her and some originating with me. We eventually figured out how to support, love, and care for one another in the middle of the worst moments of her life, but it wasn't easy or pretty.

We fought. She at times felt overlooked and like I wasn't helping enough, and I at times felt like I was loving the best I could with little capacity for more in my life. We weren't a picture-perfect representation of how you walk the worst together, but our love and commitment didn't wane. Life is hard. Sometimes it takes away things we love, and we are forever left with a hollow, gaping hole. Experiencing grief and suffering with a friend may be some of the hardest roads we walk, and we see this reality play out in Job's story.

Friend Elihu, who was younger than the rest and had remained silent out of respect for the others, speaks up in a big way. He calls out each of the men, Job included, and angrily corrects them. Elihu calls out Job for thinking he was justified rather than God, and he calls out his three friends because they didn't correct Job and still condemned him. Yikes! Job has been experiencing the worst weeks of his life, and now he is in a major tussle with his best friends. When life kicks us to the ground and we are trying to process it all, we can sometimes lash out at the people who love us the most. But the three friends who have a lot to say haven't been counseling Job with Godly wisdom. When everything in our life crumbles around us, we need friends that are wise. Seek out those women for your inner circle and fight hard to keep them once you have them.

Then we see the Lord call out Job and his friends, He speaks to them in a whirlwind, perfectly representing His anger with them. God and Job wrestle with some heavy stuff, a reminder that we can all take our stuff to God and sort it out. Eventually Job submits to God, saying "but now my eyes have seen you" (Job 42:5). As this story nears the end, we see Job interceding in prayer for his friends. The friends that had just mocked him and tortured him in his suffering are the same friends Job prays for. These friends submitted to the instruction of the Lord and sacrificed as God commanded, and then Job prayed for them. There is immense power and love in prayer, and I want to make sure we don't gloss over the significance of praying for friends. God specifically told Job to pray for his friends, and anytime God speaks in the Bible, we need to perk up and take note.

In verse 10 we read,

> *"After Job had prayed for his friends, the Lord restored his fortunes and gave him twice as much as he had before"* (NIV).

That is a powerful prayer!

This story serves as a beautiful reminder that we can have our scuffles and disagreements and still maintain healthy friendships. These friends sat with Job when he was at his worst; they showed up and did the hard things. They empathized with him, they comforted him, and they were there in his time of need. We also see how they screwed up in that time of need, and yet, through prayer and Godly instruction, they restored what was broken.

As we seek out relationships and friendships rooted in God, we are reminded that this is less about us. We can enjoy our coffee dates, girls' trips and pedicures, and all the laughter and fun, but we also need to wholeheartedly encourage our friends. We encourage them when life is knocking them down. We encourage them when they've lost sight of our amazing God. We send them memes to make them laugh. We pray abundance and kindness over them. We deliver takeout when they need it. We drop everything and rush to the hospital. We show up without makeup or a cute outfit and clean their toilets. We apologize and pray when conflict won the day. We speak life into them and genuinely hope the best for them.

We do the uncomfortable, and we do the fun. We invest wholly in trudging with them through the murky swamps and the gorgeous mountaintops that make up life. The reward is well worth it.

READ > ANALYZE > APPLY

Read Job 1 through 2 and 42 with me.

› Does anything stand out to you? Do you have questions you would like to research further?

› How and what did Job's friends do to encourage him? Note that here. How could you apply these same actions to your friendships?

› Read Job 42:7–9 again. How can this passage translate to life within the body of Christ today? List out practical steps.

› What does this passage model for us in regard to friendship? Is there something specific that you feel convicted to improve in your response to your friends? Do you have a friend, past or present, with whom Godly instruction and prayer would be beneficial? Take that to the Lord right now.

Week 4
Day Four

Learn

"...if you have any encouragement from being united with Christ, if any comfort from his love, if any common sharing in the Spirit, if any tenderness and compassion, then make my joy complete by being like-minded, having the same love, being one in spirit and of one mind. Do nothing out of selfish ambition or vain conceit. Rather, in humility value others above yourselves., not looking to your own interests but each of you to the interests of others." Philippians 2:1–4, NIV

Challenge

As we pour into themes of friendship this week {Kingdom, grace, encouragement, love + prayer, and servant heart}, let's pray about how well we rank in each theme. Are there any that you think you do well? Any that you could improve upon? Are there any tangible or practical next steps for those benefiting from improvement? If so, spend some time moving forward with those steps and enhancing the way you love and friend.

| LOVE + PRAYER |

Many years ago, I was greatly wronged by someone, leaving me bloody, raw, and bitter straight through to my soul. As I worked on forgiveness, healing, and moving forward, it became clear that I needed to start praying for this person. In total honesty, I didn't want to, but this experience was my first real glimpse into the power of prayer. I chose to pray anyway, clunky and barely-there prayers, but then something amazing happened. My heart started softening, the pain became less sharp and intense, and my prayers for this individual became truly genuine and heartfelt. Today I can say with all honesty that I wish nothing but the absolute best for this person. At a certain point, the process of forgiveness and healing required spiritual intervention through prayer, not only for the other person but also for me. It seems illogical, but it was the ultimate salve for my healing wound.

In Luke 6:28, Jesus tells us to "pray for those who mistreat you." Have you ever prayed for someone who harmed you? If we are to pray for our enemies, the people we dislike very much, then what do you think this means for our friends?

I am minorly obsessed with sitcoms and constantly find myself referencing them in relation to life experiences. Most of the time, nobody around me knows what I'm talking about, but if you spend any amount of time with me, you eventually will hear me excitedly talk about that sitcom moment that is so like this or that.

In the show **How I Met Your Mother**, Ted Mosby is sharing with his teenagers the long and drawn-out story of how he met their mother. In one of the episodes, he mentions the baggage all people bring to a relationship with the screen showing all the women he's dated while varying suitcases and trunks pop onto the screen. This scene so aptly captures each of us in life, not just our dating lives. We each carry around the pain and hurts of past experiences, and it becomes the filter through which we encounter life. Even when we have a solid relationship with God, this filter can be askew, but this is where prayer steps in. Prayer allows us to love outside of our own limitations and baggage. When we are lifting others up to Christ, our hearts can't help but soften to His will for them.

I was studying Paul's letters to the church and the prayers and encouragement he offers them. Did you know that he mentions prayer blessings 31 times, specifically wishing them God's grace, peace, mercy, and love?! It's so important to note, too, that many of these were written when Paul was imprisoned. He even asks them at times to "remember [his] chains" (Colossians 4:18). When Paul himself was suffering, he was encouraging and praying for his brothers and sister in Christ.

We can spend all the time in the world encouraging our friends, loving our friends, offering our friends grace, and helping them strengthen their faith walk; but if we aren't praying for our friends, then we are missing a key piece of Christian love. According to the NIV Exhaustive Concordance, the word pray is used 125 times in the Bible, not including various conjugations of the verb. After the word pray, prayed is mentioned 68 times, prayer 106 times, prayers 33 times, praying 36 times, and prays 9 times, for a grand total of 377 times. That's a lot!![3] As we have poured our time into friendship and loving others selflessly and sacrificially, how does prayer fit in? When we are broken and our filter is askew, prayer is the lens that corrects it. I

---

[3] "Pray." NIV Exhaustive Concordance. Zondervan Academic, 2015.

underwent a pretty extensive surgery a couple of years ago, and it left me with plenty of scar tissue. The crazy thing about scar tissue is that it adheres to anything and everything around it for the purpose of healing a wound, and oftentimes the body changes and adapts how it moves with the new scar tissue.

Each and every one of us, even the strongest of Christians, have scars on our lives, and even when we heal, something about us moves differently. It can be polarizing and divisive to not understand the actions of another. Sometimes others do something with zero malice or ill intent, but that's not how it is perceived. This is when we need God's wisdom to intervene so that we may respond with grace, and that requires prayer. He perfectly knows the hearts and intentions of all.

Through prayer and connection with God, we are aligned with God's perfect love for the other person. I believe it is one of the most amazing ways to love others and is truly

 foundational to Godly friendship. If praying for others, including friends, is something new to you, I encourage you to baby step your way into praying for someone else. We will never be able to love another exactly as God does; His love is pure and Holy. But we have the gift of the Holy Spirit and a direct line to heaven, so let's use it to friend well!

Pray for God to show you His heart for your friend and ask Him to show you how to love her abundantly as He does. Can you imagine what would happen if every single one of the women reading this study took their heartache, frustrations, and conflicts to God, rather than gossip, fighting, and causing division? Let's throw off the sin and discord that so easily entangles (Hebrews 12:1), lift our eyes heavenward in prayer, and radically love the world. Women linked arm in arm in prayer are a powerful force that the devil cannot shake. Let's be unshakeable!

READ › ANALYZE › APPLY

Read 2 Thessalonians 2:16–17, Ephesians 1:15–19, 2 Corinthians 13:13, 1 Timothy 1:2, Jude 1:2, and Philippians 1:3–6.

› After reading all of the verses above, what stands out to you?

› How do Paul's prayers in these passages connect to his frequent blessing of Christ's grace, peace, love, and mercy?

› What do these passages teach in regard to praying for the church or friends? How can you apply this to your life today?

› Take time right now to pray for your friends.

Week 4
Day Five

LEARN

> *"...if you have any encouragement from being united with Christ, if any comfort from his love, if any common sharing in the Spirit, if any tenderness and compassion, then make my joy complete by being like-minded, having the same love, being one in spirit and of one mind. Do nothing out of selfish ambition or vain conceit. Rather, in humility value others above yourselves, not looking to your own interests but each of you to the interests of others." Philippians 2:1–4, NIV*

CHALLENGE

As we pour into themes of friendship this week {Kingdom, grace, encouragement, love + prayer, and servant heart}, let's pray about how well we rank in each theme? Are there any that you think you do well? Any that you could improve upon? Are there any tangible or practical next steps for those benefiting from improvement? If so, spend some time moving forward with those steps and enhancing the way you love and friend.

| SERVANT HEART |

Today we are going to dive deep into the heart of it all, the servant heart. When you think of the friends in your life, are you able to look past her brokenness and see her beauty? Do you feel jealousy or envy when thinking of her? Do you desire the best for her, or does some part of you hope your life is always just a little bit better? Do you wish you could have her stunning home, fancy car, or over-the-top poolscape? Or maybe you wish for a husband like hers or kids like hers? Are there any sharp edges or cracks in your heart for your friend?

If each of us is brutally honest with ourselves, I think we would find some hard and less-than-pretty answers to the above. This is not because we are horrible people but because most of us want the best for ourselves. It's human nature. My prayer as we continue to process biblical friendship is that we are pruned past much of the above. Wouldn't it be amazing to see a friend and never think or feel "UGH" again but rather feel genuine joy for her? My heart's cry is to wish abundance and blessing on the women in my life, regardless of my current circumstances. Even when I'm desperate to be seen and heard but feel invisible. Even when my greatest dream is floating between us but no hope for it is returned. Even when she doesn't meet me where I want her to. If I know that she loves me, then I lean into the best for her anyway. We will always be fighting sin nature and all that brings, but we have the perfect example of a servant heart on full display throughout the Bible. Jesus offers so much insight into loving and friending well.

Let's read John 15:1–17 today.

Verses 12 and 13 leave no wiggle room for "ugh" moments.

> *"This is my command: Love one another as I have loved you. No one has greater love than this: to lay down his life for his friends." John 15:12–13, CSB*

Over the years I have poured my time into nonprofit work, some of it offered audience and exposure, but much of it was behind closed doors doing some rough stuff. I will never forget the first time I entered the projects to do a cleanup of an apartment building. The hallways were littered with used needles and condoms. The apartment kitchens were caked with old food and grease piled so high it was evident cleaning never happened. There were varmint droppings and bug infestations. Nothing about the work was glamorous. It was hard and dirty work. It would have been easy for those of us helping that day to judge the ways of these tenants, puffing ourselves up with the knowledge that our lives aren't this out of control.

But could any of us really compare ourselves? Before Christ grabbed hold of my heart fully, the condition of my life looked much like that of those tattered and grimy apartments. It needed all of the bleach and scrubbing possible, but God offered more than a little bleach and elbow grease... He offered me life everlasting with Him. I no longer have to live in the grime and piled on dirt of my sin life; I get to wear the pure white of Christ. Knowing how great a gift that truly is, my life's purpose is to share that gift of love with the world around me, including the beautiful women in my life.

Sacrificial love was paramount to all that Jesus did. He spent His entire life ministering to the world around Him, knowing that He would receive nothing in return. Nothing. His desire for us to know Him and experience eternal life was more valuable to Him than any other reward. He sought out and served the least of these: the sinners, the tax collectors, the prostitutes, and the contagiously sick.

> *"For I was hungry and you gave me something to eat; I was thirsty and you gave me something to drink; I was a stranger and you took me in; I was naked and you clothed me; I was sick and you took care of me; I was in prison and you visited me. …. Truly I tell you, whatever you did for one of the least of these brothers and sisters of mine, you did for me." Matthew 25:35–36, 40; CSB*

This offers beautiful insight into how we love like Jesus and a perfect blueprint for how we friend.

In John 15:15, Jesus says,

> *"…I have called you friends, because I have made known to you everything I have heard from my Father" (CSB).*

Jesus had knowledge that was special and unique. He had access to the Father that we didn't have, yet rather than keep it to Himself, He spent His days sharing it with all those He encountered. Do you model this level of generosity in your relationships? I think that because it's Jesus, we sometimes overlook the fact that He was human. He had the same temptations that we do, and His innate human nature might have very much enjoyed being the exclusive keeper of the knowledge of God. That would wield some serious power, and He could have made an uber glamorous life for Himself, but He didn't. Because He had perfect knowledge of our Heavenly Father, He was able to withstand temptation and selflessly serve the world. Sit in this for a moment…. Jesus knew God, He knew the heart of God, and He knew the passion and purpose of God. Because Jesus knew God, He could endure the hardships of a sacrificial life and ultimate death for you and me. This makes me want to KNOW God will all of my being.

Do we love this sacrificially? Do we lay down our lives for our friends? I don't mean that we physically die; there are opportunities aplenty to lay down our lives for our friends, to die to ourselves for their sakes. It's pretty much a given that a friend will call in crisis when you are at your most tired, drained, and empty. In that moment, there is a choice: do I give only to the point that is still comfortable, or do I give past that to the point of discomfort? This is where we are sacrificial; this is where we love like Jesus. When your girlfriend is having a rough day and calls you in distress, do you put the bra back on and meet her in her need, or do you offer words of encouragement over the phone and go to bed? While both offer support, one does so sacrificially.

More often than we realize, we are offered an opportunity to love until it hurts, but are we willing? In John 13, we see Jesus wash the feet of his disciples, a task that was far from glamorous, especially for a king, and then he says,

> *"...you also should wash one another's feet. I have set you an example that you should do as I have done for you" (John 13:14–15, NIV).*

Would you wash your sweet friends' feet? Feet that are traipsing around in grimy flip flops, mud under the toenails and caked on the soles, almost black from all that dirt. Would you? I wouldn't want to, but the real question is, would I anyway?

We have the gift of a God that walks with us through our lowest of lows, offering us love and support as we keep trying to put one foot in front of another. He is wholly committed to us. Even when we make poor choices or ignore Him, He never leaves us. The God of the universe who created you and me invites us into an intimate and personal relationship with Him. But unless we are intentional and pursue Him on purpose, none of this really matters. The same applies to relationships with our sisters in Christ. We can gain so much community, connection, and support from these relationships, but without intentionally pursuing and loving them, none of it really matters. In Ephesians 1:6–7, Paul talks about the *"glorious grace which he [Jesus Christ] has freely given us in the One he loves"* because *"In Him we have redemption through His blood, the forgiveness of sins, in accordance with the riches of God's grace"* (CSB). Jesus sacrificed to the point of shedding blood, modeling for us just how much He loved us. And when we deserved none of it, He forgave us in the most beautifully gracious way possible. Does this pierce your heart with the truth of how to friend? Can we, as mere humans, love like Jesus?

It is by grace that we have been saved, not of ourselves but as a gift from God (Ephesians 2:8–9). Our posture in friendship should be to model the same grace, loving sacrificially and serving our friends with a Christ-like servant heart. With Jesus as a barometer for friending well, we have our work cut out for us, but with our eyes fixed heavenward, we can love in the most challengingly beautiful way. Let's brave the hard and love with all we have in us.

READ > ANALYZE > APPLY

Read John 15:1–17.

> What stands out or speaks to your heart from this passage?

> What is commanded in these verses? Take time right now to pray about your own heart in reference to these commands.

Read Matthew 25:35–36.

> Write down the actions referenced in these verses. Highlight any that you would like to work on.

> What from today's study stands out to you? Did God prompt your heart with anything? Pray about your desires for your friends and ask God to open your eyes to how He sees your friends.

Week 5

WISDOM UNLOCKED

INTRODUCTION

This week of study is going to look a little bit different as we wind down our time studying **Sweet Friendship**. We've been deep in the studying of sacrificial love and relationship, hopefully challenging us in our walks with God and with our friends. Rather than diving deeply into more, we are going to take some time to sit and ruminate on what we've learned. Sometimes we invest in these amazing Bible studies but get to the end and find that we never took the time to meditate on what we were learning. We don't want that to happen here; we want to finish the last page of this study and feel confident in how to friend in the best way possible.

VERSE

"The discerning heart seeks knowledge, but the mouth of a fool feeds on folly." Proverbs 15:14, NIV

CHALLENGE

Each day this week will offer unique challenges as we go deeper into all we have studied to this point. Invest in quiet time and prayer as you allow God to show you where and how to take what has been taught here and apply it to your life. Let God lead you to fulfilling relationships rooted in Him and allow Him to prune your heart to glorify Him in your friendships and life.

Week 5
Day One

Learn

"The discerning heart seeks knowledge, but the mouth of a fool feeds on folly." Proverbs 15:14, NIV

Challenge

Each day this week will offer unique challenges as we go deeper into all we have studied to this point. Invest in quiet time and prayer as you allow God to show you where and how to take what has been taught here and apply it to your life. Let God lead you to fulfilling relationships rooted in Him and allow Him to prune your heart to glorify Him in your friendships and life.

| Kingdom | the eternal kingship of God, the realm in which God's will is fulfilled

Thank you so much for journeying with me through **Sweet Friendship**. It has been a joy to study Scripture with you and share life in this way. This is just the beginning of steps toward abundant and beautiful relationships, of friendships rooted in Christ and His purposes.

I know all too well that when Bible studies offer days of reflection, it is easy to skip them or skimp on them. It's maybe even possible that I have been guilty of that before, but I urge you to take the time today. These pages right here are where we take what we've learned and make it personal. This is where we go from knowledge to life change.

Read Proverbs 15.

Did any verses tug at your heart? If so, make a note of them in the margin and date it.

Did you notice any verses in relation to Kingdom focus in our friendships? In **Sweet Friendship**....

We studied Jonathan and David and their covenant relationship before the Lord.

We looked at Ruth and Naomi and saw how Naomi was influential in Ruth finding God.

We read about Daniel, Shadrach, Meshach, and Abednego and how together they stood firm for the Lord.

We found Joseph trusting God that his hardship was for good.

We saw Job and his friends submit to the Lord.

We were challenged by Paul encouraging and praying for his brothers and sisters in Christ.

And we saw how everything that Jesus did pointed us towards Kingdom living and relationships.

Was there anything we studied that you wanted to spend a little more time on? Maybe something you wanted to read again or study further? Take some time now to go back to anything you didn't have time for.

When it comes to Kingdom-focused living, knowledge, wisdom, and truth are paramount.

We desperately need Christ at the center of all our relationships.

> *"The lips of the wise broadcast knowledge, but not so the heart of fools." Proverbs 15:7, CSB*

> *"The tongue of the wise commends knowledge, but the mouths of fools pour out folly." Proverbs 15:2, ESV*

Take some time now to pray and journal about where your heart is in relation to Kingdom living.

Prayer journal about your focus, view of Kingdom living, and Kingdom focus in your friendships.

Use this time to pray for your friends, for what God is revealing to you, and for any next steps.

Week 5
Day Two

LEARN

"The discerning heart seeks knowledge, but the mouth of a fool feeds on folly." Proverbs 15:14, NIV

CHALLENGE

Each day this week will offer unique challenges as we go deeper into all we have studied to this point. Invest in quiet time and prayer as you allow God to show you where and how to take what has been taught here and apply it to your life. Let God lead you to fulfilling relationships rooted in Him and allow Him to prune your heart to glorify Him in your friendships and life.

| Grace | free or unmerited favor, blessings

I know all too well that when Bible studies offer days of reflection, it is easy to skip them or skimp on them. It's maybe even possible that I have been guilty of that before, but I urge you to take the time today. These pages right here are where we take what we've learned and make it personal. This is where we go from knowledge to life change.

Read Proverbs 15 again today.

Did any new verses tug at your heart? If so, make a note of them in the margin and date it.

Did you notice any verses in relation to grace-filled friendships?

In *Sweet Friendship*...

We were encouraged by Jonathan and David and their love-filled grace for one another despite complicated circumstances.

We saw Joseph do what seems impossible and offer grace and forgiveness to his brothers who intended to harm him.

We read about Paul's heart for the church and his prayers of grace and peace to all. Was there anything we studied that you wanted to spend a little more time on? Maybe something you wanted to read again or study further?

Take some time now to go back to anything you didn't have time for.

When it comes to loving well, grace is a central and crucial ingredient. Because we received such abundant grace from Jesus, we are challenged to offer the same sacrificial grace to all we encounter.

> "The heart of the righteous weighs its answers, but the mouth of the wicked gushes evil." Proverbs 15:28, NIV

> "A quick-tempered person stirs up dissension, but one who is slow to anger calms a quarrel." Proverbs 15:18, NET

Take some time now to pray and journal about where your heart is in relation to grace-filled living.

Prayer journal about the current state of your heart.

How often do you forgive?

How can you multiply grace in your friendships?

Use this time to pray for your friends, for what God is revealing to you, and for any next steps.

Week 5
Day Three

Learn

"The discerning heart seeks knowledge, but the mouth of a fool feeds on folly." Proverbs 15:14, NIV

Challenge

Each day this week will offer unique challenges as we go deeper into all we have studied to this point. Invest in quiet time and prayer as you allow God to show you where and how to take what has been taught here and apply it to your life. Let God lead you to fulfilling relationships rooted in Him and allow Him to prune your heart to glorify Him in your friendships and life.

| Encourage | give support, confidence, or hope to (someone)

I know all too well that when Bible studies offer days of reflection, it is easy to skip them or skimp on them. It's maybe even possible that I have been guilty of that before, but I urge you to take the time today. These pages right here are where we take what we've learned and make it personal. This is where we go from knowledge to life change.

Read Proverbs 15 once again.

Did any verses tug at your heart today? Note them in the margin and date it.

Did you notice any verses in relation to encouraging others?

In *Sweet Friendship*….

We studied Jonathan and David's friendship filled with encouragement and support for one another.

We looked at Ruth and Naomi and saw how Naomi encouraged Ruth to find all God had in store for her.

We read about Daniel, Shadrach, Meshach, and Abednego and how together they encouraged one another to stand firm in extreme adversity.

We found Joseph encouraging his brothers despite their ill-treatment of him. We saw Job's friends encourage him as they sat with him in his lowest of lows.

We were challenged by Paul encouraging and praying for his brothers and sisters in Christ.

And we saw how in everything that He did, Jesus encouraged us to love like Him.

Was there anything we studied that you wanted to spend a little more time on? Maybe something you wanted to read again or study further? Take some time now to go back to anything you didn't have time for.

As friends, we have the unique privilege and power of speaking life into those we love. The words of a friend can buoy us up or drag us down. Let's compliment the work God is doing in her life and offer her abundant life-giving love in all you do.

> *"A happy heart makes the face cheerful, but heartache crushes the spirit." Proverbs 15:13, NIV*

> *"The cheerful look of a messenger brings joy to the heart. And good news gives health to your body." Proverbs 15:30, NIRV*

Take some time now to pray and journal about where your heart is in encouraging and speaking life into your friends.

Which friend needs encouragement right now?

Prayer journal about your heart towards your friends and how you can encourage them in their lives and their faith walks.

Use this time to pray for your friends, for what God is revealing to you, and for any next steps.

Take a minute and write out a prayer for the friend that comes to mind. Then send her a text message to let her know that you just prayed for her.

Week 5
Day Four

Learn

"The discerning heart seeks knowledge, but the mouth of a fool feeds on folly." Proverbs 15:14, NIV

Challenge

Each day this week will offer unique challenges as we go deeper into all we have studied to this point. Invest in quiet time and prayer as you allow God to show you where and how to take what has been taught here and apply it to your life. Let God lead you to fulfilling relationships rooted in Him and allow Him to prune your heart to glorify Him in your friendships and life.

| Love + Prayer | feel deep affection for (someone)

I know all too well that when Bible studies offer days of reflection, it is easy to skip them or skimp on them. It's maybe even possible that I have been guilty of that before, but I urge you to take the time today. These pages right here are where we take what we've learned and make it personal. This is where we go from knowledge to life change.

Read Proverbs 15 again.

Did any verses tug at your heart? Make a note of them in the margin and date it.

Did you notice any verses in relation to loving our friends?

In *Sweet Friendship*...

We read about Daniel, Shadrach, Meshach, and Abednego and how together they prayed.

We found Joseph sacrificially loving his brothers.

We saw Job and his friends love and care for one another.

We were challenged by Paul loving and praying for the Church.

And we saw how everything that Jesus did was done with love.

Was there anything we studied that you wanted to spend a little more time on? Maybe something you wanted to read again or study further? Take some time now to go back to anything you didn't have time for.

When it comes to loving our sisters in Christ, prayer is such a powerful tool. As our hearts lean into that connection with God, His love flows through us.

> *"Whoever heeds life-giving correction will be at home among the wise."* Proverbs 15:31, NIV

> *"The discerning heart seeks knowledge, but the mouth of a fool feeds on folly."* Proverbs 15:14, NIV

Take some time now to pray and journal about where your heart is in relation to loving and praying for your friends and sisters in Christ.

What does your prayer life look like currently?

In conclusion,

Friends,

Thank you so much for journeying with me as we studied Biblical friendship. I hope by now you can see the beauty of relationship rooted in Christ and the value of a selfless and loving heart towards our friends. Just because we have put in the time and learned more about friendship doesn't mean that we will always have perfect relationships that never falter. Over time your friendships will ebb and flow; you may even lose some in horrifically painful ways. And sadly, it can be the relationships we thought were the gold standard for friending. No matter the state of friendships in our lives, we can still choose to love like Christ. We can pray, offer grace, forgive, and love, whether up close or from a distance. And let me remind you that you will always have access to a friend that will never leave or abandon you. When the whole world walks away, and it feels like there are no friends to be found, when loneliness and isolation become your today, Jesus will still be right there with you. Loving you, choosing you, and encouraging you in who He knows you can be. He invites us to love like Him and friend like only He could. What a beautifully sweet friendship that is.

Sweet Friendship Cupcakes

CUPCAKE INGREDIENTS

1 1/4 cups all-purpose flour
1/2 tsp salt
3/4 cup sugar
2 tsp pure vanilla extract

1 1/4 tsp baking powder
1/2 cup unsalted butter, softened
2 large eggs, room temperature
1/2 cup buttermilk, room temperature

CUPCAKE INSTRUCTIONS

1. Preheat the oven to 350°F and line a cupcake/muffin pan with cupcake liners.

2. In a medium bowl, whisk together 1 1/4 cups flour, 1 1/4 tsp baking powder, and 1/2 tsp salt. Set flour mix aside.

3. In the bowl of an electric mixer, beat butter and sugar on medium-high speed 5 minutes until thick and fluffy, scraping down the bowl as needed.

4. Add eggs one at a time, beating well with each addition then scrape down the bowl. Add 2 tsp vanilla and beat to combine.

5. Reduce mixer speed to medium and add the flour mixture in thirds alternating with the buttermilk, mixing to incorporate with each addition. Scrape down the bowl as needed and beat until just combined and smooth. Divide the batter evenly into a 12-count lined muffin or cupcake pan, filling 2/3 full.

6. Bake for 20–23 minutes at 350 °F, or until a toothpick inserted in the center comes out clean. Let them cool in the pan for 5 minutes, then transfer to a wire rack and cool to room temperature before frosting.

Frosting Ingredients

1 cup (226 g) unsalted butter, room temperature
4 cups (456 g) confectioner's sugar, sifted to remove lumps
1/3 cup (76 g) heavy cream, cold

2 teaspoons vanilla extract
1/8 teaspoon salt
1/4 teaspoon almond extract, optional

Frosting Instructions

1. In a large bowl, add room temperature butter and beat with a hand mixer (or stand mixer) until creamy, about 1 minute.

2. Add confectioner's sugar and slowly mix until ingredients are fully combined. Then, whip at high speed for 2-3 minutes, or until light and fluffy.

3. Add heavy cream, salt, and vanilla extract (and optional almond extract) and whip for an additional 3-4 minutes, or until light and fluffy. Add additional heavy cream as needed to reach desired consistency.

4. Pipe or spread frosting with a knife onto cupcakes and serve.